BREAKING DAD

HOW MY MILD-MANNERED FATHER BECAME BRITAIN'S BIGGEST METH DEALER

Withdrawn from Stock

JAMES LUBBOCK
with **WARREN FITZGERALD**

MIRROR BOOKS

First published in hardback by Mirror Books in April 2019

This paperback edition published in December 2019

Mirror Books is part of Reach plc
10 Lower Thames Street
London EC3R 6EN
England

www.mirrorbooks.co.uk

ISBN 978-1-912624-49-2

Typeset by Danny Lyle
DanJLyle@gmail.com

Printed and bound in Great Britain by
CPI Group (UK) Ltd, Croydon, CR0 4YY

A CIP catalogue record for this book is available from the British Library.

Every effort has been made to fulfil requirements with regard to
reproducing copyright material. The author and publisher will be
glad to rectify any omissions at the earliest opportunity.

1 3 5 7 9 10 8 6 4 2

Cover design: Blacksheep Design Ltd

For Jo, Mia, Gracie, and Mum

CHAPTER 1

EARL GREY

'Let's go for dinner at that lovely French place. Just me and you.'

'What's the occasion, Dad?'

'Oh nothing, just—'

'What?'

'I have some news, and… I'd rather tell you over dinner. OK, I have to go, son.'

'OK.' He was gone already. '…Bye.'

I never liked surprises – not in real life, anyway. Twists in thrillers, horror films, sci-fi curveballs, that's all fine, that's fun. Edge-of-the-seat drama, pitch-black haunted mansions with an evil ghoul hiding just off-screen, demonic girls hobbling out of unplugged TV sets – all good. I relished the escapism, the adrenaline rush of being scared witless. But in real life, I was always uncomfortable with uncertainty, even if I knew the surprise was going to be a good one. A girlfriend once planned a birthday party for me and refused to let on what it was all about. For the next month I put on a grateful smile to mask my gut-wrenching anxiety. When the big day finally came, it was revealed to be a retro Scalextric party – a genius idea for a tech nerd like me – but I had spent so many sleepless nights worrying about what it could be, I barely had the energy to enjoy it. (And if I'd known, I would have been able to get in some valuable practice time and perhaps even won the tournament rather than finish an agonising second, but that's obviously not the point.)

So when I got to the bistro, my stomach was already full from anxiety, twisted with the nervous tension of not knowing what was coming, leaving no room for the delicious food on offer. My appetite remained unwhetted as I watched an unusually nervous Dad fiddling with his favourite soup starter, though the large glass of white wine I'd ordered was a welcome anaesthetic against any terrible news Dad was about to deliver, and it was disappearing fast.

'I've never seen traffic like it!' Dad said – he had kept me waiting for three quarters of an hour, which was pretty normal for him. 'Nice decor,' he said, admiring the Roman numeral clocks of all shapes and sizes that adorned the walls, the name of the restaurant being hammered home at every opportunity – La Bonne Heure.

The irony was not lost on me.

'Nice ambience. There's a good vibe about this place,' he said, smoothing the red and white gingham tablecloth between us.

Vibe? Since when did my dad use words like vibe? Was he trying to be cool? It really didn't suit him.

'Mmm,' was all I managed while my brain chattered: *Bloody hell, he's going to tell me he has a lovechild.*

'The service is always really good,' he said. 'You don't mind tipping well when the service is good, I've always said that.'

'Mmm.' I said again. *He's got a terminal illness. Oh my God, he's going to die, I knew it!*

Between the small talk he was chowing down on his fingernails more than he was on the onion soup, continuing to unsettle me. As the first half hour wore on, Dad's behaviour became increasingly alien – he looked unsure of himself, kept hesitating, clearly unable to pluck up the courage to tell me his revelation. It was unnerving. You see, I'd always thought of Dad as superconfident, in his slightly eccentric way; assured, certainly in front of me at least; a well-travelled, successful businessman, who was never, ever lost for words. Yet here he was, a bag of nerves, and I couldn't bear it anymore.

'Come on, Dad, spit it out!'

He looked aghast, wondering for a second whether I meant the spoonful of broth he'd finally slurped up. But as soon as he realised I was talking about his news, he swallowed, took a large draught of his water and said, 'OK, well, the thing is… I'm… Well… Back when I was at school, I… started getting these feelings… for boys.'

All those clocks on the walls stopped.

3

I think Dad carried on talking at this point, but I didn't really hear the words he said. I just heard my own brain screaming round my skull: *Well, you didn't see that one coming, did you, James, old bean!* Out of all the things it could possibly be, my dad being gay was probably bottom of a list of a thousand possibilities that had been scrolling through my head for the last excruciating half hour. After all, he couldn't be gay, because how could he and Mum have had me if he wasn't interested in women? Oh God. Perhaps *I'm* the lovechild. Wait! Perhaps I'm not his son after all, perhaps… No, my dad wasn't gay. He was a ladies' man, everyone said it and I had seen it all my life. OK, he was no alpha male, that's for sure, he was the quintessential English self-deprecator, in fact, but women flocked round him. *Because he was no threat to them, you twat, that's why they flocked*. OK, he was a little camp, now I thought about it, but so is Mick Jagger. *You mean Mick Jagger, lead singer of the Rolling Stones, who was once caught in bed with David Bowie?*

Shit! My dad's as gay as a *Sound of Music* singalong, and everyone could see it except me.

But in actual fact, it was nothing like that. As I focused on what he was saying, I realised he had simply been suppressing a genuine part of himself – a part that he was afraid I would be ashamed of, a part that he was afraid the world would be disgusted by – for many years. He grew up in an era when being gay was not only commonly held to be a sin, but it was also, incredibly, against the law. So he'd tried

4

to be 'normal', get married, have kids, like everyone else did, like you are *supposed* to.

And so, mixed in with the shock, I felt a sudden surge of sympathy for him and a strange sort of happiness that, after all these years, he could finally be true to himself. He didn't have to hide this significant part of himself anymore, and he didn't have to lie to friends or family. He could live life to its fullest at last.

The main course was so much more palatable than the starter, the Bolognese flavoured by the bizarre buzz of speaking to Dad as an equal, as an adult, for the first time. That felt good, and I suddenly felt grown up, as if I had come of age so much more than I ever had when I was *supposed* to: at my bar mitzvah, for example, or my first day at university. So I found myself saying grown-up things like:

'I'm happy for you, Dad.'

And: 'You're still my Dad, whatever you do.'

Little did I know how that one would come back to bite me in the arse soon enough.

Then I asked, 'Does Mum know?'

'Yeah, for a few weeks, but she wasn't surprised when I told her,' he said, adjusting his glasses in a manner I could only describe now as camp, when a few minutes ago I would have seen it as simply nervous.

'Do you have a boyfriend?'

'No,' he said through a mouthful of breadstick. 'I don't think I really want a relationship or could have another one anyway.'

'OK, but are you being safe?'

'Safe?'

Oh God, now I knew what my parents felt like when they tried to have that birds-and-bees conversation with me years ago and I told them not to be so embarrassing. 'Yeah, you know,' I said and found myself gesturing to the breadstick in his hand for some reason, 'condoms and stuff.'

'Oh! Yes, but you know it's not as much of a risk as they say.'

He smiled reassuringly, but that was the one answer I didn't like the sound of at all.

I remember that short walk back from dinner more than any of the other countless ones I took along Abbeville Road in Clapham during the three years I lived there – or Abbeville Village, as the pretentious twats that populated the place liked to call it. It certainly felt like a life-changing moment, not just for Dad, but for me too. And although the summer air and the smells coming from all the other cafes and restaurants were as comforting and delicious as ever, and the constant chatter and clinking of plates and cutlery were as vibrant as always, I was unfamiliar with the world, uncertain of the future.

Will and Jake, my flatmates, were gagging to hear what the bombshell was, so much so that they even paused *Getaway* on the PS2 to find out.

'Well, what did he say?' Will asked, looking up expectantly.

Jake was on his feet and hovering in the background, his usual excitability heightened further by unbearable anticipation.

'Well,' I said, 'I didn't see that coming.'

Jake laughed nervously as he scanned my face for a clue.

'What?' Will stood up. 'You've got a long-lost sexy sister who's my age, single and ready to mingle?'

'No.'

'Well, spit it out!'

I smiled wryly; Will sounded just like me an hour or so ago.

'OK,' I said, executing some long Pinteresque pauses for dramatic effect. 'Are you ready for this?'

Will and Jake nodded like a pair of panting cocker spaniels.

'My dad just told me…' Pause. 'He's gay.'

Jake tutted. 'Very funny. What did he really say?'

Jake had known my dad since we were both thirteen, for over ten years. Dad had taken me and Jake to Arsenal matches when we were kids. The dad that Jake knew, as did I, was a run-of-the-mill, mildly eccentric, but ultimately ordinary, clichéd Jewish dad. He had a conservative approach to life, didn't like smoking or drinking, and viewed drug-taking as one of society's ills. At our suburban home in North-West London, he enjoyed reading the *Daily Express* over a cup of Earl Grey tea, complemented with a couple of Rich Tea biscuits. If he was feeling adventurous, he would sometimes dunk the biscuits in his tea. His favourite TV programme was the *Six O' Clock News* on the BBC. He repeated his favourite jokes ad nauseam.

Case in point: every time Mum asked him to put the kettle on, he protested that it wouldn't fit him. I heard that one alone literally thousands of times. He was passionate about classical music and opera, visiting the Royal Opera House regularly, cajoling me a number of times to accompany him to the latest production of *Aida* or *Figaro*. He often fell asleep on the sofa, stroking his protruding tummy (the result of one too many salt beef sandwiches), after a hard day's work dealing gold coins at his Dickensian shop, squeezed between a boutique selling Indian saris and a Polish travel agent on Regent Street.

Ever the businessman, he liked deals, however seemingly insignificant they were: he'd enjoy spending an hour hunting round Tesco until he'd landed the best bargain on cereal – then he'd regale anyone who was listening with the details of this momentous consumer triumph. He'd drive to the other side of London to get the best deal on petrol, saving himself an incredible 1p per litre at his chosen petrol station, apparently oblivious to the fact that he spent a whole lot more on fuel just getting there. And then there was his never-ending excitement around finding the optimal parking space during those shopping excursions – there was nothing he liked more than relating the tale of how he spotted, with eagle eyes, the prime bay and quickly nabbed it, reverse parking his trusty Ford Cortina in one smooth move, no corrections, within yards of the entrance to the target shop.

His infamous plastic carrier bag was another fixture Mum would be constantly rolling her eyes about. Each bag would be used until it fell apart, and would include critical items such as his asthma inhalers, five Kleenex tissues carefully folded in a stack, his diary, keys, the day's newspaper and another spare plastic bag in case the current one decided to finally give up the ghost that day.

He enjoyed watching some sports, especially our football team, Arsenal, but he would never do anything more sporty than playing table tennis, partly because of his asthma, and partly to help perpetuate the stereotype that all Jews are shit at sport.

Yes, my Earl Grey dad was a steady, predictable dad – a safe foundation on which to build a family.

'He can't be gay,' said Jake, running a hand in confusion through his mass of brown hair, or Jewfro, as we liked to call it.

I shrugged. 'He is now.'

'Has he got a… boyfriend?' Will smirked.

'No, he doesn't seem interested. I have the feeling he's… experimenting,' I said, cringing slightly.

'Jesus,' Will concluded. None of us really knew what to say. 'Fancy a spliff?' he added.

It was starting to sink in – I had a gay dad. That's cool, right? I thought. Suddenly I had a story, an anecdote, something that made me a bit different, more interesting. You could say I was almost a bit edgy now. Almost.

'This is big news,' said Will. 'We need to roll one up.'

Jake was gobsmacked but, by means of a brief nod, concurred with Will, as did I – this indeed warranted the rolling of one massive spliff.

CHAPTER 2

GOULASH

A few days later I went out for dinner with my mum, presumably to chew the fat over this bombshell, support each other through this unexpected turn of events. And I was sure she would be the one needing more support than me. After all, although they'd been separated for a few years now, she had effectively just lost her husband for good, and not to another woman, from whom you could potentially win him back. No combination of Ann Summers lingerie and romantic candlelit dinners could possibly win a wife her homosexual husband back, no matter how much brisket you served.

So my Mum chose this celebrated little Hungarian restaurant in Soho called The Gay Hussar. I know! The relevance of the name was not lost on me, but little did I know just how that name was about to be seared onto my brain for eternity. We sat down and ordered some goulash – probably – since nearly everything on the menu was some kind of goulash, be it veggie goulash, beef goulash, goulash pancake or goulash soup. There might have even been goulash sundae for dessert, but it all gets a bit hazy after the main course. And then we got chatting. Dad being gay was pretty high on the list of topics for me, obviously, but Mum didn't seem too fazed by it. In fact, she seemed to be quite happy about it and, just as I was about to ask her why she wasn't devastated, she said: 'So, *I* have some news, James.'

'Yeerrrs?' I'm thinking, now what? I can't take any more of these fucking bombshells, you know I hate surprises at the best of times.

'Well, you know Dad's news?'

'Yeerrrs.'

'And you know I've been living with Ruth for a bit now.'

'Yeerrrs.'

'Ruth is my girlfriend.'

'Yeah.' Bit of a strange Americanism my mum chose to use about her friend: *girl*friend, I thought. It seemed an unnecessary prefix, adjective or whatever it was (hey, I'd just finished Media Studies at an ex-poly, not English at Oxford), but nothing shocking in that, I thought.

I suppose Mum saw I was still oblivious, and gracefully put me out of my ignorance. 'It's more than just friendship. Ruth is my lover.'

The goulash arrived.

Mum picked up her spoon. 'I'm gay too,' she smiled.

I burst out laughing. I mean, she had to be joking. Didn't she?

CHAPTER 3
SHAKEN AND STIRRED

When monumental things happen like this (do monumental things ever happen quite like this?), you tend to rewind through your memories and try to find the 'turning points' (as we used to say in the film studies module of my degree), or the moments when you might have seen it all coming. Certainly my parents splitting up during my first year at university was a bit of an 'inciting incident' (as we also said on the course) on the journey we were all about to undertake. Throughout my childhood and teenage years, I knew it wasn't the happiest of marriages, but that was all marriages, wasn't it? I witnessed many long, drawn-out arguments, Mum not speaking to Dad for days on end, then thankfully *détente* and, for me, a huge sense of relief that this wasn't the end of the relationship. I remember it was generally Mum being the unreasonable one, the one giving the silent treatment. However, while my dad was a charming guy without a bad bone in his body, I knew Mum found him exasperating at times. He had these habits that grated, slowly driving her up the wall until she exploded over something relatively minor. Yet at the same time they shared a wicked sense of humour, which seemed to me essential survival gear for a relationship. So when I left for Bournemouth University, I hoped that with their only son out of the way, their relationship would enjoy a renaissance of romance, laughter and, although it turned my stomach to think about them at it, sex.

They separated after only one term.

I arrived back after that first term to find them at each other's throats in a way I hadn't seen or heard before. I think I was on the phone to Jake at the time.

Jake was in the USA. His parents had emigrated to Atlanta when we were both sixteen. I was gutted at the time, but luckily we never lost touch and our friendship became even stronger as a result, despite the messy leaving party where we got him steaming drunk, chased him out onto the street, stripped him and tied him to a lamp post naked. He hung there looking like an inebriated Jesus Christ but, as ever, took it in incredibly good humour. Even as we lashed him to the lamp post, a man walking his dog called out to him, 'Are you OK, son?'

'Oh, fine,' he shouted with a massive grin. 'They're my friends.'

'So how's life at Bournemouth Poly?' Jake scoffed down the phone.

'It's a uni.'

'Poly.'

It *was* a polytechnic just a few years before, but, 'A rose by any other name would smell as sweet,' I said, feeling very erudite as I recalled something from a history of Shakespeare in cinema lecture.

'A shite by any other name would smell as bad,' countered Jake, recalling something from the University of Life which he insisted he attended, but which I was sure was in fact nothing but the Regional College of Remedial Studies of Life.

'How many birds you shagged?' he asked.

'Oh… Well… I… I've lost count, mate.'

'Yeah?' Jake wasn't convinced.

'Oh yeah, you should see the birds down there. They're all super-hot and totally up for it.'

'Really?'

'Yeah, I've barely got any work done. Virtually every night I go down the union bar, bring a different girl back to my room and bang her senseless over the washbasin.'

'Bullshit,' Jake observed.

I didn't contradict him because the reality, of course, was this: drink one bottle of cheap, demi-sec white wine and two cans of Tennent's Extra Strong to achieve the required level of Dutch courage before heading out; schlep to the Fire Station (that was the imaginative name they gave to the students' union bar because it was once, you've guessed it, a fire station); sail in there full of myself – tonight's going to be the night, lads; go for my first 'wander' round the club, looking for girls – but not any old girls of course, ones that were on my course so I could open with a question about our latest assignment or something equally dazzling; epically fail to engage any girls in decent banter; end up hanging out with my new mate, Will, at the bar, 'people-watching', you know, generally becoming increasingly drunk and bored; eventually go back to my room, where the only thing I did over the washbasin was throw up, resulting in me having to spend the morning with a banging head picking pieces of Pot Noodle out of the plughole.

I was never the most confident of chaps, socially speaking. In fact, you might say I was a bit of geek. I'd been to an all-boys' school and girls still scared the crap out of me when I arrived for my first year at Bournemouth, where my student digs were so very generously, and it turned out rather optimistically, furnished with a double bed – the droves of beautiful women I imagined I would woo there never materialised. I don't suppose my wardrobe helped much – and I'm talking about my dress sense now rather than the furniture. It was a mixture of my mother's somewhat retro choices for her 'little soldier', and mine, which were mainly driven by a desire to imitate James Bond – the Roger Moore version. So I would proudly go out on those nights down the Fire Station in tight white jeans, with one of a selection of polo-neck jumpers in a variety of loud colours, or my 'smart' clothes for things like the summer ball, which made me look like a cross between a waiter and Pee-wee Herman. And for some reason the girls still didn't flock! So most of the time I found myself propping up the bar with Will, trying to nod my head in time to 'Smells Like Teen Spirit' and ordering a martini, shaken, not stirred – because that would make me look cool, right?

'You what?' the barman shouted the first time I ordered it.

'Martini, shaken, not stirred,' I shouted back over the noise.

'You mean a *vodka* martini?' the barman screwed up his face as if I'd just let one go and wafted it over the IPA pump at him.

'Er,' I stammered. Is that what I meant? Did James Bond have vodka in his martini? I suddenly realised I had no idea what a martini, shaken, not stirred really was. The barman was looking more impatient than ever. It was now or never. Say something, you dick, before he turns to someone else and it takes another half hour to get served. 'Er, yeah, yes please.'

The barman muttered to himself as he turned, and it was as if every student stopped talking in that instant and the juke box paused simultaneously, just long enough for everyone in the whole world to hear him grumble, 'Twat.'

So instead of those thrilling nights in the union bar, I was usually more than happy to stay in my room on the PlayStation or watch *Star Trek* or read Asimov. As I said, I was a bit of a geek, and when I arrived home after my first term at uni, I was still an actual virgin. It was so humiliating. I mean, no one else I knew was a virgin. Or at least no one else I knew let on that they were anyway.

'You need to shower a bit more before you'll ever need the proverbial shitty stick, mate,' Jake laughed down the phone.

'I do shower. Just not very often. The communal shower's got weird things growing in it.'

'You still got that greasy curtain hairdo? That's so 1990.'

'So? Still got a Jewfro?'

Well articulate after a term at university, me.

'Bloody hell, what's going on there?' Jake had heard the row going on in the background.

'Just the parents arguing again.'

'Can't you go somewhere quieter?'

'The phone cable's not that long.'

'Don't you have a cell phone yet?'

'A what?'

Before he could enlighten me, my dad's voice roared down the hallway. 'Shut up, shut up!'

And then my mum's. 'Call yourself a man? You're not a man, you're pathetic.'

'You fucking bitch, how could you?' he screamed at her.

'Hey, mate, everything all right there?'

I went red even though Jake was a million miles away.

'Yeah. I'll call you back later though, OK?'

'OK, mate. Erm, take it easy, eh?'

'Yeah,' I said, hanging up and rushing upstairs to the safety of the cyber world inside my PlayStation. I'd never heard my dad lose it like that, ever.

*

The next day we went together to see Arsenal play. As we watched David Seaman boot the ball all the way from the six-yard box to Ian Wright up front, Dad said, keeping his eyes on the ball, 'Your mum and me, well, there's a chance we could be splitting up.'

There's a chance. So it's not for definite. *There's a chance.* That's all I heard, all I wanted to hear, so I roared with the rest of the supporters as Wrighty hit the bar.

'You should apologise to Dad. You didn't need to speak to him like that.' I tore into Mum before tearing into my burger.

For her birthday on 30 December, I had taken Mum out to this relatively new restaurant, Planet Hollywood, which was then in the Trocadero in London. Come to think of it, given that the Trocadero was this massive gaming mecca and Planet Hollywood was all about movies and burgers, I'm not sure my motivation for choosing this venue was particularly selfless. But I wasn't in a selfless mood anyway. I felt defensive. I felt like I was fighting for my solid little family unit's life.

'You can't take sides in this, James. It's not my fault the marriage is over. It's a decision your dad and I have both come to.'

The marriage is over. That's all I heard. Not *there's a chance we could be splitting up*, as Dad had said a few days before on the terraces at Highbury. It was over. There was no ambiguity in Mum's words, just finality. That was that. It was New Year's Eve tomorrow and it began to sink in that I would be starting 1997 as a child from a broken home. OK, I was nineteen, hardly a child anymore, but it didn't stop it really sucking balls.

CHAPTER 4

GOLLUM IN A TANK TOP

So Mum moved in with her *friend*, Ruth, and Dad sold the family home in Stanmore. Ever the eagled-eyed businessman, he bought some flats with the proceeds in Limehouse, East London, not just because they were great investments, and not really because Limehouse had been the centre of the Jewish community back in the day, but also because Limehouse had a thriving gay community at that point. However, I was still ignorant of that fact, as I was of Dad's new-found sexuality.

He had in fact bought four flats on the top floor of this brand-new build. He moved into one and planned to rent out the rest, but for now the one next to his was just stuffed with relics of his former life, from furniture which once filled the old house to piles and piles of VHS video tapes. The flat he lived in was sparse by comparison. The laminate wood-effect flooring in the huge open-plan living/dining/kitchen area was sprinkled with just a few stools, and the magnolia walls were devoid of any adornments, except for one collage of Freddie Mercury – yes, all the signs were there. Perhaps I should have sussed it sooner, but actually I was a fan of the rock band Queen, so I simply admired the collage instead of getting all Lloyd Grossman and asking myself, 'Who lives in a house like this?'

After all this time he had still not properly moved in, it seemed, as there were piles of half-opened boxes in the corners of all the rooms, full of kitchenware, bric-a-brac and clothes.

The box room, funnily enough, was perhaps the only room without boxes in it. Here Dad had moved his office. He had given up the Regent Street shop, realising it was an unnecessary overhead. He had also been the victim of an armed robbery there not long ago and this had put him off, not surprisingly. It was enough to put anyone off, let alone my straight-laced, law-abiding Dad.

This new office did hark back to the one in the West End, though. It was just as cramped as the corridor of a room he'd had on Regent Street. Both had a desk in the middle (with a telex machine back then, a PC now) and a chair either side, one for Dad and one for the client. Both were lined with filing cabinets, books on numismatics (that's coin dealing to you and me) and piles of papers. And both were attended by his faithful secretary, Diane. Diane had been working with Dad for over twenty years now. I even remember sitting on her knee as a kid and drawing on old carbon copy paper as she worked, her voice a soothing coo above my head. 'No one knows the business like Diane,' Dad would say proudly.

There were two bedrooms in this new flat. Dad's was sparse, grubby, with papers strewn around. There wasn't even a proper bed in there, just a mattress on the floor. It was a rather sad-looking room, but there were echoes of his previous life here too: just by the bed all his 'essentials' were as neatly laid out as ever – diary, clothes, water, tissues and his Tesco carrier bags containing his inhalers. Nevertheless, to a student like me, it was a pretty cool bachelor pad, so I couldn't wait to show Will, who had come to stay with me at Mum's during summer break.

I buzzed the intercom.

'Dad?'

'Oh. James. It's you.' There was a pause, as if he had put his hand over the receiver and spoken to someone inside. Then, 'Come up!' The lock buzzed and I pushed through the heavy door.

When we reached the flat, Diane opened the door with a warm smile and told me to hang on: Dad was just winding up some business in the office. This was not an unusual situation for me. Ever since I was a kid I was always waiting for Dad to finish some business before he got to me. And I felt like that little boy now, impatiently hanging around his desk, eager for him to finish what he was doing with his associates so he could take me out to the toy mecca of Hamleys or McDonald's for a large portion of fries.

Will and I hovered in the living room and chatted with Diane, who was getting ready to go home. We heard Dad jabbering away as he always did with clients – his business was very much a social one. The coin dealing itself was a minor point in the proceedings. Or that was how it seemed. Back in Regent Street he was always on the phone. He had two landlines then, two old rotary dial phones, and he would sometimes be on both simultaneously. He would even hold the two receivers together and tell each caller to say hi to the other in this hilarious precursor to Skype. Dad was a connector. He liked people to get on well with him and each other. And it was strong business sense: if you have a good sales experience you'll buy and come back for more.

His coin-dealing business had been handed down to him by his father. And at one point he had wanted to pass it on to me. 'One day all this will be yours, son.' But I wasn't interested, and he'd accepted that. However, I was soon to inherit a whole world of something from him that I never would have dreamt possible.

Eventually the door to the office opened and Dad showed his client – a beefy bloke, swarthy and well dressed in an expensive-looking suit – to the front door.

'Afternoon.' The guy smiled at me and Will.

'Hi,' we chorused.

And, just before the office door swung shut, I caught a glimpse of that desk with the PC where there had once been the telex machine and those two rotary dial phones; of that desk with electronic weighing scales where once there had been mechanical ones; of that desk with a large bag of grass where once there had been antique coi—

Hang on! Grass? What the fuck?

'See you, boys!' Diane sang and followed the suited bloke downstairs.

'So, boys,' Dad said, closing the front door. 'Cup of tea?'

'No thanks,' Will said, 'but I'm dying for a wee, can I use your toilet?'

'Sure. Down the hall, on the left.'

Will scurried off.

'James?'

'Mmm?' I was still more than a little distracted by that vision on Dad's desk.

'Tea?'

'Oh, no, we just popped in to say hello. Then we're off to a house party.'

'Oh cool.' Dad nodded.

Cool? Since when was my going to a house party *cool* with my dad?

'I'm going with some friends to The Fridge later. You and Will should come too, after your house party.'

The Fridge? This must be the name of some new haute cuisine restaurant, probably one that only served vichyssoise, cold cuts and salads. I mean, it certainly couldn't be the nightclub in Brixton, could it? So I sought the necessary clarification. 'The Fridge? What's that?'

Dad laughed a little scornfully. 'Come on, you know. That club in—'

'Brixton?'

'That's the one. Friday nights are great down there.'

Friday nights? Like he's been before, and on more than one occasion? How can this be? Who is this man before me? Since when did my dad go to nightclubs for... 'What music are they playing tonight?' Beethoven? Brahms?

'Hard house mainly. A bit of trance.'

A bit of trance? I didn't need a cup of tea, I needed a stiff drink. But of course, Dad was teetotal, so there'd be nothing in the flat to quench this discombobulation I was experiencing. I'd just learnt that word after one of those conversations in the communal kitchen at uni – you know the ones, where you nod knowledgeably for an hour, leafing idly through the newspaper you hope best represents the political leanings of the cleverest bloke in the room, then run off to find a dictionary at the earliest opportunity to try and find out what the hell everyone was going on about. Of course, I never thought I'd have a use for such a pretentious mouthful, but right then in Dad's open-plan kitchen-diner, I couldn't think of a better word to describe my feelings.

Will came back from the toilet just then and, since I was not able to articulate a coherent response, Dad asked him instead. 'Will, how about it? The Fridge tonight?'

'The nightclub?'

Dad nodded.

'With you?'

Dad nodded again.

'Yeah, OK,' Will grinned.

I punched him, of course, and said 'Er, no thanks, Dad.'

'I mean, who goes clubbing with their parents?' I said as I sipped a *vodka* martini in the kitchen of the house party we'd elected to go to instead.

'I know.' Will grinned. 'That's just it. It would've been so funny.'

'Only because it's not *your* dad.'

'Exactly. And it would be a lot more exciting than this,' he said, gesturing to the few stoned blokes talking shit to each other by the sink.

He had a point.

And so we ended up at The Fridge. And there, unashamedly pogoing about in the midst of a crowd of Brixton's *yoot*, was my now skinny dad in a tank top, the thick black curls he'd always had all gone in favour of a shaven head. The big glasses he'd always worn had remained, but it was quite a change of image from the 1970s suits and the paisley shirts that my previously chubby dad had worn.

'Oh my gosh,' Will giggled. 'He looks like Gollum.'

'Shut up,' I said through my teeth as he noticed us and waved us over.

'My precious, my precious!' Will persisted. I duly ignored him.

We pushed through the throng on the dance floor. Dad's face lit up in a way I'd never seen it light up before. He bounded over to me and gave me an enormous hug.

'Hey, Dad,' I said with a slightly nervous laugh.

'Son, you are the greatest son ever. I love you, son. Do you know that, son?'

He held on to my arms and I could feel him squeezing me like I was a Jew-shaped stress ball or something. As he squeezed, his eyes rolled back in his head. 'Wooooooh!' he squealed. 'Come and meet my friends!'

As he dragged me across the club I looked back at Will, who was wetting himself because he knew as well as I did that my middle-everything father, who had told me how disgusting smoking was, who had never had a drink in his life and thought that drugs were morally wrong and only for life's drop-outs and losers, my Earl Grey dad who had always hated dance music and told me to turn down that 'hukking' in his own weird version of Yiddish, which he liked to employ at times of particular parental indignation, had not only traded in Handel for hard house, but was lighting up a fag and totally off it on ecstasy.

CHAPTER 5

THAI WEED

The next day I felt it was my duty to go round to Dad's flat to make sure he was all right. After all, he was bound to be on a massive comedown, feeling fragile after popping his drugs cherry. Despite my Nerd Loyalty Card being stacked with points, even I had had the odd pill on my way through uni, so I knew how he would be feeling. I was feeling rough enough after all the booze I'd drunk last night just to deal with the sight of my dad on E, his arms round a load of young people closer to my age than his.

However, he was annoyingly chipper and even working. He chatted away in a bell-bright tone which rang around my pounding head as he showed another well-dressed gent, in a déjà vu of last night, out of his office.

Then I remembered the big bag of grass I'd seen last night and, as he said goodbye to the guy at the door, I poked my head

into the office to see if I had imagined it. No, it was still there.
I scampered back to the kitchen and perched on a stool as Dad
shut the front door.

'Tea?'

'Go on then.'

'Dad?'

'Mmm?'

'Did I see a massive bag of drugs on your desk?'

'Ah.' He pushed his glasses up his nose in that nervous
manner, which I was still yet to see as camp. 'Yes. Probably. It's
just weed though.'

Smoking weed was, and is, not an uncommon pastime
among my community – it helps with the Jewish neurosis. I
was, of course, partial to the odd joint myself. But this was my
dad we were talking about. First the clubbing, then the pills,
now the smoking.

'But why have you got so much?'

His answer was pure Dad the businessman. 'You get a better
deal if you buy a lot.'

'A lot! Who needs *that* much?'

'Oh, I give it to friends too.'

Alarm bells rang – no, not in the apartment block. This
wasn't a fire drill, although my heart sank as if something I
loved dearly was going up in flames. These were alarm bells the
size of Big Ben and they were crashing against the inside of my
skull – and no, it wasn't just my hangover getting worse either.

Someone who has a load of illegal drugs and gives some to other people, isn't that the definition of a drug... I could barely hear the word over the sound of ringing; or perhaps I didn't *want* to hear the word... dealer.

Hang on! *Hang on!*

My Earl Grey dad never did things by halves. I mean, look at all the reduced-price cereal in his cupboards! This was just my dad being his eccentrically logical self. As the man said, you get a better deal if you buy a lot. The only thing that would make him a dealer would be if—

'Dad, are these friends *paying* you for it?' I said, gesturing to the front door. The guy in the suit who had just left had not seemed the nerdy numismatist type – and I guessed he was one of those friends Dad was talking about.

'No, no, no.' He shook his head. 'Even if... even when I give some away, I still save money on that much. Daddy got a very good deal.' He giggled.

That little *Play School* impression tagged on the end did not amuse me, but as he spoke of savings as if we were simply standing in the aisles of Tesco, the bunch of Big Bens banging in my bonce were wrapped in thick, downy duvets of doubt, and I gave him the benefit of it. Oh, they still rang furiously for a while, but I just couldn't... wouldn't hear them anymore. After all, it was only weed.

'Do you want some?' he said.

Do I want some? Since when does someone take weed off their middle-aged dad? That would be so uncool. That would make it seem almost acceptable and that would kill the buzz of illicitness which enhances the high itself.

But it's only weed.

'No charge, of course. Whenever you need some more just let me know.'

The bells were doing their damnedest to break free of their fluffy shrouds.

It's only weed. And it's free weed at that!

The bells were silenced.

'Yeah… OK… Cool,' I heard myself stutter and I stared agog at the back of Dad's shaved head shining in the beams from the recessed lighting as he bounced off to the office to sort me out.

So I spent the rest of my university days trying to keep up with my dad, but no matter how hard I tried, those nights propping up the union bar with a vodka martini looking like a cross between Roger Moore and Shaun Ryder could never compete with my fifty-nine-year-old dad's tales of all-night raves, submerged in the new wave of dance music culture in the club capital of Europe.

But at least I was no longer a virgin. Dow had seen to that.

It was on one of those riveting nights at the Fire Station, and I was going around picking up discarded-looking fag packets, in the vain hope that there would be a couple of abandoned cigarettes inside needing a home, when I heard a voice, cutting through the din like a strangled duck.

'Hey, you!'

It came from a group of Asian-looking girls. One of them was beckoning me over to sit down next to her. I dutifully obeyed, of course.

'What is name?' she squawked.

'Me?'

'Yes you.'

'Oh, me. I'm Lubbock. James Lubbock.' I thought I heard the barman's voice in my ear going 'twat' again, but I shook it off and said, 'And you?'

'Sasithorn Sonjohnkoksoong.'

Oh shit, I thought. 'Erm… Pardon?' I said.

'Sasithorn Sonjohnkoksoong.' Then she grinned a beautiful white grin and added, 'But I called Dow for short.'

'Thank God,' I muttered. 'Nice to meet you, Dow,' I said, returning her grin. 'Where are you from?'

'Thailand. Phuket.' (It's pronounced *Poo-ket*, by the way.)

'Wow,' I said, 'That's… erm… a long way from here.'

What a line, my brain laughed derisively. *That's sure to win over this hot Thai chick, you dick.*

As I began internally smashing myself over the head with the empty beer glass on the table before me, Dow said, apparently undeterred by my social constipation, 'You like me?'

'What?'

'You like me?'

'Erm…'

The answer is yes, you idiot, a simple, yes, not 'Ooh, well we're on the same course, I don't want to make things awkward.' You know, like you came out with to that Louise, the first girl who ever showed you any interest here.

I took a deep breath. 'Yes.' I smiled.

'You like to see me again?'

'Yes,' I said without hesitation this time.

'You take my number then.'

I turned out all my pockets in a desperate attempt to locate a pen, but only managed to unearth a receipt for incense sticks and microwave lasagne. One of Dow's friends luckily came to my rescue and handed me a biro. As I wrote the number on a beer mat Dow examined it, making sure I had got it all down accurately. When she was satisfied, she stuck her finger in my chest and quacked, 'You call me, OK?'

'OK.'

'Be sure call me, OK?'

'Definitely.'

'Are you fucking joking?' The voice of an ape shot across the table in a huff of garlic. 'You choose him over me?' said the incredulous jock, and at first glance I had to agree with him.

'Fuck off!' Dow instructed him. Luckily, with nothing more than a derisive guffaw, he did. And instead of allowing his little malodorous intrusion to piss on my picnic, I actually felt great because, as this stunningly exotic creature was making perfectly clear, she had indeed chosen me over him. And so I was happily deflowered. Yes, she turned out to be a completely nuts bunny boiler who caused me no end of grief, inciting screaming rows in public every five minutes, but you're missing the point: my cherry was popped!

At least my newly divorced old man couldn't trump me when it came to matters of a carnal nature, could he?

That was when the phone rang and he said, 'Let's go for dinner at that lovely French place. Just me and you.'

'What's the occasion, Dad?'

'Oh nothing, just—'

'What?'

'I have something I need to tell you, that's all.'

CHAPTER 6
SLEIGHT OF HAND

I made a point of visiting Mum and Dad regularly so they knew nothing had changed as far as I was concerned after they'd both told me they were gay. It wasn't far to Dad's from the flat I now shared with Will and Jake in Clapham post-uni. And that was handy, because there was another reason apart from my filial devotion for visiting regularly – and that was so Dad could get us drugs. Since I'd told Will and Jake about the weed on Dad's desk, they kept on at me to go and 'see how my dad was getting on' with unusual levels of concern for his well-being.

When New Year's Eve of 2002 came around, I had got us tickets to the Ministry of Sound event at the Millennium Dome in Greenwich. We had planned a large night, one that would require class A fuel to get us through to the early morning. The trouble was, I didn't know anyone who could get ecstasy pills. Nor did Jake or Will. As we toked one night in front of the

PlayStation on a large spliff stuffed with weed my dad had given us, images of him pogoing around a club, yes, like Gollum in a tank top, eyes wide with MDMA coursing through his ageing veins as if it were some elixir of life, floated in the smoke before me. I couldn't believe what I was thinking. Weed was one thing, but class A drugs!

I walked in on Dad trying to take a selfie with his camera when the term selfie was still only spoken by Aussie self-portrait photographers as they grabbed another tinny from the esky at a barbie.

'Take a picture of me, will you!' Dad said in frustration as he examined yet another close up of his neck on the screen of his Olympus.

'OK,' I said, taking the camera from him. 'What's it for anyway?'

'For my profile picture.'

'On what?' I said, expecting him to say numismatist.com or something.

'Gaydar.'

I nearly dropped the phone.

Although it was still a relatively new thing, since leaving uni I'd been working in digital marketing so I knew very well what Gaydar was. I just couldn't believe my dad did. Nevertheless, I proceeded to take his picture with very slightly trembling hands as he sucked in his stomach and jutted out his chin to give the camera his best side for his profile pic on this gay dating site. It wasn't the fact that Dad was looking for a date that unsettled me, it was the fact that he was, given his previous comments on not wanting a relationship, more than likely using the site to meet blokes close by for a quick hook up, as they say – which is, as I understand it, what most users did. Even in my hetero world, where my conquests still only numbered one (and that was Dow, who did all the conquering, really) I wasn't a connoisseur of the quickie. So, as you can imagine, Dad's new-found promiscuity, whatever his sexuality, was still a lot for me to take in.

'There's a few to choose from there.' I gave him back his camera. And as he examined the photos, deleting the ones he didn't like with a tut as if I was the worst photographer in the world, I had to restrain myself from saying, 'Well you can't polish a turd, Dad.' Somehow I managed it and instead muttered, 'Erm, Dad?'

'Mmm?' he said, still absorbed in the screen.

'Is it possible for you to, I mean, if you can get hold of any…'

He looked up as I stuttered around the subject.

'What do you need, son? Spit it out!'

I spat it out. 'Pills.'

'Ecstasy?'

'Yep.'

And he said without hesitation, 'Oh, no problem. How many do you want?' He jumped down from his stool at the breakfast bar and I thought for one jaw-dropping minute that he had a sack-load of pills next to that bag of weed on his desk. But he was merely retrieving a scrap of paper with a number scrawled on it from the top of the microwave, which he proceeded to dial into his phone.

'How many, James?' he repeated nonchalantly as if he was dialling Pizza Hut and confirming my garlic bread order.

'Erm. Well, it's for me, Jake and Will—'

'They're pretty strong,' he said with bizarre authority, 'so two each will be plenty, but we'll get nine just to be safe.'

To be safe? What was safe about getting extra narcotics? And why was I worried about safety all of a sudden? And why was my dear old dad giving *me* advice on the potency of in-vogue street drugs?

'His name is Alfie,' Dad whispered as he waited for Alfie to pick up. 'Was in prison but recently released. Harmless though, got done for possession, I think.'

'Oh,' was all I could muster.

'Alfie? Alfie, it's Richard. I'm great thanks, mate. Just wondering if you could hook my son up with some sweets.'

Sweets? Was that code so whoever was tapping the phones was thrown off the scent? Because a grown man often calls another grown man asking for some Haribo, don't they? Jeez, Dad!

He continued, 'Can you do us a deal on ten? Nice. OK. I'll let him know. His name's James.'

You didn't think a code name was necessary for me then? I could have been Double O Eight, licensed to pill. Or not.

Apparently I was to meet Alfie (if that was his real name, which I had a sneaking suspicion it was) in a pub down the road the following evening at six o'clock. I'd never met a dealer before and I almost asked Dad to go for me, but things were getting weird enough already – it was about time I, er, grew up and grabbed the mantle of unruly teenager back from my middle-aged father.

At six the next evening I entered The Magpie public house trying to banish the old rhyme about the bird from my head: *One for sorrow, two for joy.* Why couldn't the pub have been called The Two Magpies? I hesitated at the door for a very uncool and protracted second until I noticed the bear standing by the bar. When I say bear, it wasn't the sort of cuddly one with a shiny yellow jacket and a pork pie hat that you saw propping up the bar in the ads for Hofmeister lager in the late eighties. This bear looked more like Hagrid from the Harry Potter films, the second of which had just been released and which I had of course rushed to the cinema to see along with all the other nerdy children in the world. And, like Robbie Coltrane's interpretation of the Hogwarts' caretaker, this hairy giant looked like he could rip your head off with one flick of his massive wrist, and yet his eyes were gentle enough to stop me from turning round and scurrying back to the safety of the warren of city streets beyond the pub.

Alfie – for it was he – raised his bearded chin in my direction, beckoning me over with it. And I, not wanting to risk decapitation, obeyed.

'James,' he growled warmly, holding out his shovel of a hand.

'You must be Alfie,' I said, hating the tremble I heard in my voice as I shook the proffered appendage.

He began making small talk about how lovely a fella my old man was and I managed to respond, I think, but I was totally distracted by the sensation of a small plastic bag of pills in my hand, which he had somehow deftly planted there during the handshake. I was both impressed by his sleight of hand, especially for a hand anything but slight, and terrified that I was already in possession of the contraband, already a sitting duck for the feds when they came crashing through those doors any moment now, which of course they were bound to, this having all the hallmarks of the most notorious drug deal in recent history.

I didn't know what to do with my laden hand. I scanned the room quickly as Alfie went on about what a good man my father was and, deciding the coast was clear, I shoved the pills into the inside pocket of my jacket. I was desperate to examine them before I did so, but I knew that would be a very uncool thing to do. It would make a mockery of Alfie's discretion if I started waving the bag about and inspecting the pills for quality – as if I knew anything about how to authenticate them anyway!

Now, as Alfie and I were quickly running low on things to talk about, I had to work out how to get the cash to him, and fast. Handing him the notes in plain sight may have been the best way, just like that guy at the other end of the bar handing his mate a tenner for the next round, but in my naivety I assumed I had to do so in a manner which equalled Alfie's awesome stealth and dexterity.

As the conversation dried up, I fiddled with the bank notes, trying to wedge them in one palm like a five-year-old attempting a magic trick. Eventually the sight of me doing this must have been too painful for Alfie the Bear to bear and as he said, 'See you around then, mate,' that hand of his swooped in and shook mine, removing the notes as if it were a vacuum cleaner – probably a Dyson or something similarly high end.

I squeaked my goodbyes and stumbled out of the pub, relieved to be leaving The Magpie behind me, but buzzing as I scampered home, a pocket full of pills, feeling like the man who can, having just sorted New Year's Eve for the boys. And as I speed-walked through East London I began to revel in the unexpected perks of having a dad who did drugs.

CHAPTER 7

SPICE GIRLS AND SOCCER STARS

I sat in the car toking on a spliff (contents supplied by Dad, of course), working up the courage to go inside.

'If booze is Dutch courage, what do you call this?' I asked Beth.

No, Beth wasn't a girlfriend. She was just a friend – like I thought Ruth was to Mum before Mum enlightened me over goulash at The Gay Hussar. I'd met Beth at Bournemouth University. When I applied for halls of residence there before I started, we had to fill out a questionnaire. There was one pivotal question in it and, at that point, I had no idea of its significance. That question was: *Do you smoke?* What I didn't realise at the time was the uni did not have enough space to house all of the students itself, so to make up the shortfall, it subsidised tired, creaking, 1970s-looking hotels in the area. And as soon as you admitted to being a smoker, you were condemned to live in one of those with all the rest of the polluters. And there were plenty of us, because the ban on smoking in public places was still just a twinkle in the Chief Medical Officer's eye and the sign of a good night's clubbing was the stench of stale smoke on your clothes the next afternoon when you woke, all alone in bed with nothing but a slimy sock stuck over your shrivelled knob for company – OK, that last bit was probably just me.

As it turned out, these crumbling *Fawlty Towers* sets were a positive place to reside. Suddenly, in addition to the immediate social group you had within your course, here was another completely random group of people whom you were going to get to know very well thanks to your common interest in pulmonary self-harming.

I was one of the first people to arrive at my hotel, but the following night most of the other students began to arrive. While I was in my room blu-tacking posters of *Trainspotting* and Nirvana above the bed (leaving the *Star Trek* and Queen ones under it, with a mournful sigh), which, in the unlikely event of a fellow student visiting, told them that I was both literary and edgy, and arranging my toiletries on the washbasin (praying that the Lynx effect actually existed), I heard the door opposite me open and the eager trills of someone moving in. To my excitement, it was a girl. I was living opposite an actual girl. What an opportunity, assuming she was my type, of course. Like I had a choice! Let's face it, if she was breathing, that would be my type. So once her family had said their goodbyes and left, I decided to do the neighbourly thing and knock on her door. She cheerily popped her head out and said hi, and even invited me in. We chatted for half an hour, just getting to know each other, you know, me keeping her at bay with a shitty stick, that sort of thing. Actually, I immediately took a liking to her, but as I did with most girls at this time, I felt like an awkward little boy.

Then, after she told me how much she hated Nirvana and I'd made a mental note to flee to my room and rip down that 'edgy' grunge crap defacing my wall as soon as possible and stick to my glam rock guns in future, she said, 'Have you got a girlfriend?'

Oh my God, she's asking me out. Already! Well, what do you expect, James, my boy? It's that Bond-smooth charm of yours, they can't resist. 'No,' I said expectantly. 'You?'

'Yes,' she melted. 'Brad. We've been going out for years. He'll be coming down next weekend. I'd love you to meet him.'

'I'd love that too,' I lied so hard. *Brad!* Even the name reeked of muscles and long blonde hair and perfect skin and white teeth. I went back to my room and binged on *Star Trek* videos.

But as Beth and I slowly got to know each other better – it was inevitable, being neighbours – we gradually became more fond of each other and more comfortable spending time together. Ultimately, it blossomed into a strong friendship, resulting in us moving into a flat with two other friends in second year. Until then I didn't even know you could have a girl as a mate without wanting to jump into her knickers and yet, although Beth was attractive, I didn't see her in that way.

I wanted to show her off to my mum, nonetheless, mainly because I knew they would get on. In fact, I was surprised I hadn't introduced them sooner, when we were still at uni. Beth was intelligent and witty and Mum would love her. I was looking forward to sitting back and watching them interact. But visiting Mum in her new home meant meeting Ruth for the first time – another reason why I'd brought Beth here. It helped that Beth was a woman, of course. I didn't feel like I could take Will or Jake into this situation – not for the first meeting anyway. They were bound to sit there like a couple of Semitic squirrels struck dumb by the headlights of homosexuality, with the added full beam of *that's James's mum!* blinding them, desperate not to speak in case, 'I suppose you just never found the right man, eh?' or even worse, 'Do you miss cock?' came tumbling out.

'Mexican courage?'

'What?' I muttered distractedly.

'Mexican courage,' Beth repeated. 'Perhaps this is called Mexican courage. They grow a lot of weed in Mexico, don't they?'

'Mmm. But by that token you could call it Attics of Hackney courage.'

'Then again,' Beth said as I passed her the joint, 'booze doesn't come from Holland exclusively, does it. Actually, I believe the term Dutch courage is something to do with the gin the English saw the Dutch soldiers drinking before a battle. And since the Dutch kicked arse, the Brits thought the gin was the reason.'

I told you she was intelligent.

'If we smoke any more,' she added, 'we won't be able to get up the stairs.'

I looked at her, imploring her not to do it, but she stubbed out the joint and opened the car door. 'Let's get this over with, eh?'

I closed my eyes in a quick prayer to the God I didn't believe in as Beth came round and opened my door too.

'Come on, mate!' I opened my eyes and looked up at her warm smile. 'It'll be fine.'

Ruth was a successful city executive and had done very well for herself. As such, she was able to afford a plush, elegant flat in the heart of Hampstead. It was part of a block of flats on a hill that overlooked North London at its leafy best.

We approached the gates and the security guard there looked us up and down with disdain, which I think it was in his job description to do to anyone who wasn't a resident.

'Hi, we're here to visit Ruth and Marilyn.' I felt myself redden as I announced to this meathead bouncer that my mum was one half of a female (and therefore *lesbian*) couple that resided in the flats he patrolled. They could be a couple of old maiden aunts, sisters even, I told myself, looking after each other in their dotage. But then again, who am I kidding, I thought as he waved us through. He would have seen Ruth coming and going in her dungarees stretched to capacity around her bulldog butch frame. Studded ears, probably one through her nose and a shaven head as sharp as her tongue. My heart sank as the lift raised the rest of us to the third floor where Ruth was bound to have a man cave of a flat.

When we came out of the lift, we almost crashed into Mel C from the Spice Girls, who it turned out lived in the same block as Ruth and Mum.

'Hiya,' she chimed before eschewing the lift for the stairs – of course, she was *Sporty* Spice after all.

'Did you see who that was?' Beth said in a loud whisper bursting with excitement.

'That one from All Saints, wasn't it?' I said in a vain effort to appear less star-struck than Beth.

She punched me playfully as we reached Ruth's – and now my mum's – front door.

I stood there looking at it with a glazed discomfort I'd usually reserve for a Jackson Pollock in the Tate. Eventually Beth rang the bell. I felt like I was in the lift again as the blood rushed to my feet.

The butch, studded, buzz-cut lezzer opened the door. Except no butch, studded, buzz-cut lezzer stood there. Instead there was an elegant woman with curly black hair and smart, rather formal, business-like clothes. She had a kind face and greeted us a little nervously. She showed us into a tasteful, homely, classy place. The carpet was cream with a lush texture underfoot, the sofa sported expensive-looking fabric, the wallpaper matched perfectly with the rest of the decor. It was spacious but not overly huge, with an open-plan lounge/dining area, a door to the immaculate kitchen, and then two bedrooms, an en suite and a study. A similar layout but otherwise quite the contrast to Dad's unloved East London place.

Ruth ushered us up to the lounge where Mum was waiting and tea was poured. Mum and Beth got on famously, as I'd hoped they would, but as they fawned over each other on one sofa that meant Ruth and I had to chat together on the other, no hiding. However, as soon as we started talking, I immediately felt at ease: we clicked, and I almost forgot about the rather bizarre situation. I felt elated that not only was I not threatened by Mum's new... her *only* girlfriend, but I liked her, really enjoyed her company.

She was originally from Philadelphia, I discovered. She had a soft East Coast American accent, was incredibly bright (a Harvard graduate, no less!), and – the cherry on the Blitz cake – she was Jewish. On occasion I saw Mum glancing over at us, searching for my approval, just as I would have done in the increasingly unlikely event of me bringing a girlfriend to visit her.

'So, you're a soccer fan, eh? Arsenal, right?' Ruth was saying to me.

'Yes.'

'Your mum and I have made friends with this guy who lives downstairs. Freddie. Apparently he plays for Arsenal or something.'

Freddie? Plays for Arsenal or something? She must have meant *works* for Arsenal, a groundsman or something. She couldn't have meant— 'Freddie? Freddie Ljungberg?' My footballing hero at the time.

'Ljungberg, that's it!' Ruth beamed. 'Do you know him?'

'No,' I gasped, 'but I'd love to meet him.'

'I'll introduce you then.' She winked. It turns out Ruth was feigning ignorance and knew exactly who Freddie Ljungberg was – she was as much a Gooner as I. This was ace! Not that we weren't getting along wonderfully before, but now I knew for sure Ruth and I were going to be great friends indeed.

'Oh, I *know*!' Beth's voice skewered my dreams of meeting the Arsenal star as she announced loudly to my mum. 'I wish I were a lesbian, life would be so much easier.'

'Oh sure,' Ruth cut in wryly. 'Except for the hate crimes, the bullying, the higher suicide rates, the work place harassment and discrimination, the possibility of being stoned to death or flogged in some countries, assault, depression, stigma, religious persecution, threats of being disowned by loved ones. Ya, except for all that, it's great.'

Did I say Beth was intelligent?

Ruth poured some more tea and I giggled at Beth's blushes. Then I smiled at Mum.

You've done well for yourself, Mum, my smile said. And I think she understood. I really hope she did. I really, really do.

CHAPTER 8

MIGHTY ERECTIONS AND MACCY D'S

Alfie the Bear's pills turned out to be consistently top quality – and I don't mean the ratio of MDMA to other substances. How the hell would I know what was in them? Top quality to me meant that nice snuggly feeling in your tummy; a fiery rush of euphoria from hugging your best mate, which in any other circumstances would be described derisively as gay; and feeling like a human balloon inflated by the sound waves emanating from the speakers you stand before, open-armed like a gurning messiah, massaged by music which it is imperative you describe, assuming you particularly liked the track that was currently playing, as a *choon*. Not a tune. On my initial forays into clubland I thought, being the university graduate I am ('Poly!' Shut up Jake!), the word *choon* was just the way the less eloquent among us ravers, those with a disinclination for RP, would say *tune*. And yet, whenever I emitted my version of the word like the bloke from the eighties' throat lozenge advert, as my current favourite floor-filler, er, filled the floor, everyone around me would look at me as if I was speaking Klingon. And when I say the pills were consistently good, I mean they were good on the few times I did them: every few months, on one of the boys' birthdays or New Year's Eve, that sort of thing.

Dad, on the other hand, was munching up pills faster than Pac-Man. Whether it was this influx of energising psychoactives into his system, the constant hopping around nightclubs, or the bedroom athletics he was engaging in, thanks to Gaydar, for the rest of his spare time, he was slimming down in ways overweight housewives gorging on packets of chocolate digestives in front of *This Morning* with Phil and Fern could only dream about. Consequently, instead of admiring his new lean figure, like a proper Jewish mum I found myself worrying that he wasn't eating enough, and every time I popped over I came bearing food.

On one occasion I decided to go round unannounced and surprise him with a Big Mac Meal. OK, it wasn't exactly brisket and apple cake, but I realised as I unpacked the fries that I was hoping for my dad's face to light up just as it used to when he saw my ten-year-old self beam at the fries he'd bought me after I'd waited impatiently for him to finish work at the coin shop in the West End.

But it didn't.

Instead he looked fidgety, impatient, anything but ready to sit and chomp on Maccy D's with his only son.

'Is Di OK?' I asked, tucking into the cold floppy chips.

I had just seen his secretary on the stairwell. The lift was out of service so I'd had to haul my hungover hide up the stairs to Dad's flat. And as I did so, Diane came rushing down them.

'Hey Di—' I'd begun.

Strangely for her, she'd said nothing, just sniffed and kept her hand over her face as if she was crying or something. I didn't have the energy to do so much as call after her to find out what was wrong. Instead I just watched her disappear down the stairwell, her short wavy hair, which had always seemed to be on the cusp of greying, suddenly looking greyer than ever. And, as it turned out, I never saw her again.

'Oh, yeah… she's… *she's* fine,' Dad said with a sad resignation which somehow suggested Dad knew he was the one who was now not OK. 'Sorry, son,' he winced, 'just finishing up with a client.' And he rushed back to his office, hesitating outside the second bedroom door for an awkward moment before deciding on the office after all.

Left to pick that horrid gherkin from my Big Mac alone, I began fiddling with Dad's laptop, which was on the breakfast bar. I pressed a random key and the screen came to life – or rather someone came on the screen. I had stumbled on a cumshot, it seemed. And not the kind of cumshot I was familiar with as I beat myself off, telling myself the girl in the film, like all the girls I was yet to meet, really enjoyed being gunged with semen. No, there wasn't a girl in sight in this porn clip, just a muscular male stomach and a very long, tanned penis, both of which, as I told myself how repulsed I was by the sight of two blokes at it, I was envious of.

It's OK, I told myself. We all watch porn sometimes – some of us more than others. And since my dad was gay now, what kind of porn did I expect him to watch?

The office door opened and I slammed the laptop shut. Dad showed his suited client to the front door and, as they passed, I waved at them both with the kind of excessive nonchalance that only the guilty have. Then the sound of men groaning floated into the room again and I thought the video was somehow still playing on the laptop, so I swung round to the breakfast bar. The laptop was silent. Yet the groaning persisted.

Dad was still chatting to the suited bloke at the front door, so I followed the sound down the corridor to the second bedroom and peered in past the door, which had been left ajar.

My pupils dilated like Dad's on E and my jaw hit the laminate as I saw three, maybe four, men (I'm sorry, I didn't hang about long enough to count properly) clad in leather – well, clad everywhere except their genitals – standing around a leather swing, which hung from the ceiling, and taking turns to bugger the naked bloke who was strapped up in it.

'James?'

'Dad?'

He quickly ushered me out onto the balcony, which had impressive views of Canary Wharf – a welcome collection of mighty erections helping to temporarily banish the others that had just been branded onto my retina. It was warm out there; the sun was shining, the birds tweeting in an atmosphere of incongruous innocence.

'I should have mentioned, there's some... friends here... for-for-for... a... meeting.' He blushed.

'It's OK, Dad,' I said, trying to hide my own blushes. I squinted at the sun and tugged at my T-shirt. 'Warm today, eh?'

'Mmm.'

'Look,' I said eventually. 'I just popped round to make sure you were OK. Thought you might like something to eat, you know. But you're obviously fine. And busy. So I'll leave you to it.'

I hurried back into the living room and nearly tripped over one of the boxes strewn about as my eyes adjusted to the relative darkness inside.

'Sorry, son.' Dad's voice came from behind me. 'Thanks for the McDonald's.'

I cursed the lift for not working, then legged it down the stairs, the spitting image of Diane a few minutes earlier, her reasons for throwing the towel in as Dad's secretary now becoming all too clear.

CHAPTER 9
MUMMY'S LITTLE SOLDIER

I found myself driving over to Mum and Ruth's place to get some normality. Well, it was as close to normal as I was going to get these days. I nearly crashed a few times as images of hairy arses bulging over faux leather chaps scudded through my field of vision. I can only thank God that my Dad's wasn't one of them, I thought, then nearly knocked over an old lady hobbling over a zebra crossing as my imagination kindly painted Dad into the sling for me, hanging from his bedroom ceiling, legs akimbo and—

My car shuddered to a stop outside Ruth's Hampstead flat. I got out and nodded to the security guard, who was by now familiar with me but, as the company handbook no doubt instructed, no less disdainful in his demeanour. This didn't bother me, however, as I already felt the tension in me ebbing away – partly, of course, due to the fact that I might bump into my footballing hero at any minute. I liked it here. Here the only surprises were likely to be Sporty Spice bounding down the stairwell or—

'An actual Arsenal shirt signed by Freddie Ljungberg!'

'Yes, it is.' Mum grinned, bringing a large tray of sandwiches and cakes to the coffee table.

I grinned too. I couldn't stop grinning, in fact, as I held up the shirt to the light as if I was trying to find a watermark to prove its authenticity.

'He was very nice about it when I told him you were such a fan. Said it was no trouble.'

'This is amazing, Mum. Thanks,' I said, giving her a big hug. Perhaps a bigger hug than usual, even. Because everything felt so right. It felt the way things are *supposed* to feel between a child and his parents. Perhaps I was too old to feel this way, but isn't that the way it's supposed to be? Parent makes tasty, nourishing food, feeds up her little soldier, gets little soldier the most incredible present, beams as little solider delights in the gift. Not: child turns up at parent's scummy flat, brings greasy takeaway with him to try and get parent to eat something, parent is too busy 'working' to eat whilst men bugger each other senseless in the next room.

Then, as if she could read all this in the intensity of my hug, Mum said, 'How's your father? Have you seen him lately?'

I grabbed a tuna sandwich and stuffed it in my mouth to stop the words from tumbling out. Then I noticed the mayo oozing from it and suddenly lost my appetite for it. I swallowed the mouthful I had with an awkward gulp and Mum, being a mum, noticed me grimacing.

'Is that sandwich OK? Did I put too much pepper on it?'

'No, it's fine, Mum,' I said, scanning the tray urgently for a different sandwich. Cheese: ew, no! Cucumber: God no! Chicken: perfect! 'It's just that I spotted one of your awesome chicken sandwiches and I can't resist,' I said, grabbing the sandwich, the contents of which were thankfully evocative of nothing but chicken, so I tucked in.

'Well, one at a time, James, no need to be a pig!'

That was right. Mum telling me off like I was a little boy; that was what I needed to hear right then. I needed to feel like a naive little kid again. She poured me some juice, but just as I was beginning to sink into the plush couch with a childlike slouch, she said, 'Well? What about your dad?' and I stiffened − no, wrong word! − I *sat up* and downed the drink to keep me from speaking just a little longer.

Mum was looking at me expectantly now. If I didn't say something right away she was going to get suspicious.

So I said, 'Oh, you know Dad.' This was a good start because of course she did know Dad. Well, lots of the old dad and some of the new. She knew he was smoking weed and clubbing a lot so I decided to keep things simple. 'He was out raving till seven in the morning the other night.'

Mum rolled her eyes. 'And what did he take to keep himself going till that early hour, I wonder?'

Mum wasn't stupid, so I said, 'Oh, that ecstasy stuff I think.' As if I had no idea what it was and wouldn't know what end of my body to stick it in if I was handed some.

'He's like a child,' she sighed and poured herself a tea. 'Where did he go? Some gay dive no doubt, full of loose men.'

The image of one particularly loose man came swinging back into my mind and I almost choked.

'You OK, James?' Mum leant over and gave me a maternal whack on the back. I was grateful for the blow, which sent the images of Dad's sex room hurtling out of my head.

'Yeah, thanks, Mum.' She didn't know just how grateful I was. Grateful that she had taken such a different path to Dad with regards to her new-found sexuality. Keeping it very subtle, in a long-term, stable relationship, living with a loving partner.

'He thinks he's the most sexually liberated person on the planet, like *the only gay in the village* prancing down the street waving his rainbow flag. He's behaving like he's twenty-one. It's pathetic really, James. I'm sorry, but it is.'

I had to agree with her. Messing around with anyone that tapped him up on Gaydar, grabbing the party lifestyle with both eager hands at his age. It was more than pathetic to me, though. It was worrying.

After a little silence, broken only by the smacking of my lips and the slurping of her tea, Mum said, 'Have you met any of his… men?'

It was all I could do not to send the last piece of chicken sandwich shooting out of my mouth and across the room, defacing that beautiful wallpaper of theirs. *Oh, yes, Mum, I have met some of his... men. All at the same time, in fact.*

'Weh-ell,' I sang, 'there are sometimes one or two of them round when I go to the flat.' *Or three or four. Sodomising each other in an S&M swing in his spare bedroom.* 'Having a drink or... something.'

Mum shook her head woefully.

The images were back, pounding my mind, and the tuna mayo sandwich remained uneaten.

CHAPTER 10

FREAKY FRIDAY

Mum and Dad were celebrating their wedding anniversary. No, this isn't another flashback. I know I'm prone to slipping into flashbacks here and there, but here's Mum and Dad celebrating their wedding anniversary in the *present*. Celebrating it as they had done every year since they split up. I know! Who does that? Well, you must have got the idea already that my parents didn't ever do the things you were *supposed* to do, at least not for the last few years since they had both come out. And I kind of liked them celebrating in this way. I liked to think they were celebrating the positives that came from all this recent madness and the good things that came out of their marriage – me, for example. That's why I liked to pop in on them during these celebrations, later on in the evening usually. I'd do so under the pretext of offering them a lift home – since my mum liked a glass or two of wine, and these days my teetotal dad, once everyone's favourite designated driver, was bound to be on something – when in fact I really just wanted to float in and present myself as Exhibit A in the case for celebrating their marriage. And as I did so at The Alpine Italian restaurant one warm, late-summer evening in 2003, Dad was just raising his glass of water to Mum's Chardonnay and toasting the real cause of their celebrations, as they saw it.

'It's been the best year of marriage so far, wouldn't you say, Marilyn?'

Mum rolled her eyes, shook her head but clinked his glass as, in many ways, she had to agree. I blushed briefly, feeling somewhat surplus to requirements, but at the same time feeling happy for them. They seemed to have become closer as a result of their separation. And that was all it was. An informal separation. Dad was, technically speaking, accurate about yet another year of marriage. They had never actually divorced.

Imbued with this sense of positivity, not to mention whatever he was on, Dad then pulled a long black wallet from his coat pocket. It had Cunard printed in red on one corner and some grand-looking tickets inside for the return trip of the *Queen Mary 2* from New York to Southampton after its maiden voyage, scheduled for early next year.

'I thought we might continue the celebration with a little cruise.' He smiled.

But Mum didn't smile. She didn't look upset either, though. She just glanced at me knowingly and then back at Dad. And after gathering the words carefully, said, 'Richard. I love you dearly, but the thought of being stuck on a boat with you in the middle of the Atlantic for seven days frankly makes me queasy.'

Dad's face dropped in pantomime proportions. 'You'd forego a once-in-a-lifetime trip with your darling husband of twenty years?'

'In a heartbeat. Darling.'

He pondered Mum's words for a moment, then looked up sheepishly. 'We'd drive each other mad, wouldn't we?' he said.

Mum nodded over the rim of her wine glass. 'That's if you even made it before the ship set sail.'

'Oh, Dad, were you late this evening?' I deplored.

He shrugged.

Mum ribbed, 'When is he ever on time?' Then added softly, 'But thanks for the offer, Richard. It really was a nice thought.'

'A bloody mental one though, eh?' Dad toyed with the tickets somewhat forlornly. He tapped them on the edge of the table as he wondered what to do with them now. He could always give them to someone else, I saw his brain tell him. But who?

I reached over him and helped myself to a piece of garlic bread.

'Son?'

'Mmm?' I said, my mouth full.

'Do you fancy it?'

I pondered it for a moment. 'But who would I take?' I said.

I could take Will – that would be a laugh. Or better still, this girl I'd started dating recently. It would be a sure way to impress her. Keep her from sussing out she was with a total dweeb for a few months longer, perhaps.

But Dad's voice interrupted my deliberations. 'Me,' he smiled.

I coughed on a shard of crusty bread. 'You?'

'Yeah. Could be fun.'

I looked at Mum. Her eyes sparkled mischievously and she pulled a face that said, *Go for it, but at your own risk!*

I weighed it up. Funnily enough, the idea actually appealed to me. Well, I'd never been on a cruise before. It would certainly be different, something new. All-inclusive, unlimited food, plus no end of amusing anecdotes to tell Will and Jake when I returned from a five-star booze cruise with my new drug-taking, trance-loving dad. It would be an opportunity for us to spend some quality time together too, for me to get to know more about this new lifestyle of his.

So I said yes, and it soon turned into a full-on US road trip too, coast-to-coast, after I received this lovely email from my second cousin Susan.

Hi James,

How are you!

All is well here in L.A. and having just returned from a business mtg. in NYC I am glad to be in warm-ish weather! Your dad told me that you are meeting him in NYC in late April to embark upon the Queen Mary maiden voyage to the UK.

As you know, your dad also is coming here to L.A. prior to meeting you in NYC for the ship to visit the Simons clan.

(As an aside, I must say you two will have a fantastic time on this adventure across the high seas and I envy you very much. I really would love to join you.)

I am writing to say that it would be just marvellous and lovely were you to come to L.A. as well.

Of course, I realise that you have work commitments that might not make a westward journey possible, especially as the sea voyage will be lengthy.

But we would just love to see you.

Even for just a few days.

I would make every effort to take time off to spend time with you and 'show you the town'.

This is especially so as at that time my family, with Richard included, will be celebrating my sister Lisa's fortieth birthday. Your presence therein would make the event all the more special and memorable.

So, this is just a gentle imploration with much affection to say that if you could swing it we (I) would be delirious with pleasure to see you again.

If not, there will always be Paris!

Lots of love,
Hope all goes well and take care,
Susan

I should point out here that Susan's (misquoted) reference to *Casablanca* refers to our mutual love of film rather than any incestuous love affair. So, now that's cleared up, how could I refuse such effusive words?

We planned to fly to the West Coast to visit Susan's family there, then traverse the entire breadth of the USA to New York, where we'd hang for a few days and then take the cruise back home. It was going to be an adventure, but just quite how it would pan out I didn't know yet, what with me now a fully-fledged adult with the freedom to do whatever I wanted in the presence of my parents, and Dad a now slightly unpredictable, more open-minded older man looking for his own type of fun.

Before I knew it the time had come and we flew to L.A. to visit the grand heads of Dad's side of the family – Susan's parents and Dad's aunt and uncle – Grace and Solomon, with whom he was extremely close, emotionally speaking. He always referred to Grace as his second mum, and in some ways felt closer to her than his actual mother. She was more dependable, emotionally stable and exuded warmth. A stark contrast to my well-meaning, but ultimately distant, lukewarm, and at times self-obsessed grandmother. Dad often blamed his relationship with his mother for many of his 'afflictions': his need for constant psychotherapy during most of his life, his inability to come to terms with the idea of death, even his asthma, which he was convinced was psychosomatic.

And now, despite having embraced his sexuality, he felt that it was at least partly triggered by this dysfunctional relationship with his mother.

So there was a deep love for Grace, and he had a steadfast respect for Solomon, a true New Yorker with an accent to match, a strong handshaker, giver of bear hugs, a powerful avuncular presence and Dad's inspiration when it came to preparing the ultimate barbecue – 'Do you remember Solomon's barbecues? They were out of this world.' He was the archetypal alpha male. So it wasn't a surprise that Dad decided not to share too much about his new lifestyle choices with him. Or Grace. Grace was like one of the Golden Girls from the eighties sitcom: sunny, bright and attractive. And she adored my dad – there was no way he was going to do anything to jeopardise that. Grace and Sol were self-confessed 'old-timers' and it was clear from the way they spoke they weren't ready to hear about Dad's sexploits anyway.

Sol: 'OK, Richard, let's get that grill on.'

Grace: 'Here you go, James, take these ribs out to Sol. They have my special sauce on them. Your son is adorable, Richard, just adorable.'

I blush.

Sol: 'Ah yes, Grace's special chilli sauce. Taste that! Does my Grace got a way with a sauce or what? Put hairs on your chest, that will, I'm telling you. Perhaps if that governor over in New Jersey had had some of this he wouldn't have turned out to be a faggot.'

I blush. Dad blushes.

Grace: 'Now, now, Sol, don't talk like that! It'll put everyone off their food.'

I blush. Dad blushes.

Nevertheless, there was something about that family. Dad, Mum and I were also very close to Susan, as you can see from her email. She was technically an even more distant relation, but she was the family member we felt closest to on both sides. There was a strong shared humour – Dad and Susan would trigger each other off in hysterics whenever they met; and as a boy, I always looked forward to seeing her. She was one of the only adults who took a genuine interest in me when I was a kid, asking me all sorts of both interesting and daft questions, making sure she spent time with me one on one, always showing me real affection. Consequently, Dad and I had no qualms about talking about his sexuality with her. Her reaction when he told her?

'I'm not surprised at all. Now what about this rock concert?'

Her nonchalance was wonderful. But then she was a respected psychotherapist and had worked with many A-list Hollywood celebrities. I'm sure she'd heard a lot worse.

And yes, what about this rock concert?

I'd managed to bag a couple of tickets to see The Darkness – my new favourite band – who happened to be playing down the road in San Diego while we were staying in L.A. (I know a two-hour drive would be tantamount to a mammoth road trip in UK terms, but San Diego really is *down the road* as far as Americans are concerned). I loved The Darkness, a British glam rock band with a strong sense of humour who were heavily influenced by Queen (my all-time favourite band), AC/DC, Foreigner and the like. Not the most fashionable mix in the Garage- and RnB-soaked early noughties, but somehow they'd managed to score huge successes with their first album in the UK and were even now making waves in the US.

'So, Dad. How about it?'

The reaction I was expecting was, 'Are you mad? Rock music? Who do you think I am? No way. It'll be far too loud. I'll get a migraine.'

But of course, that was the old dad. The new dad said, without the slightest hesitation, 'Yeah sure, why not? Let's drive down there, it'll be fun.'

I loved the new dad.

So down we drove, and I remember being genuinely excited about it all. Here was a British band threatening to make it big in the US, playing just the sort of music I loved – a very rare occurrence. And what the hell would Dad make of it? Not really his type of thing, but then neither was happy hardcore until a few years ago and now he listened to it during his breakfast.

The anticipation continued to build as we tuned into a local radio station in the car and heard The Darkness being interviewed ahead of their gig.

'Welcome to the show,' the DJ said to his guests. 'Now I have to ask you, your sound is a lot different to what a lot of the kids in our audience are listening to right now. Most of them are not even familiar with guitar solos. What advice can you give them about music?'

'Grow your hair and listen to rock,' came the goofy voice of the lead singer Justin Hawkins over the airwaves. 'Simple.'

'You heard it here first, folks. Grow that hair!' the DJ said, laughing awkwardly at these alien life forms in his studio. 'And what's your favourite guitar solo of all time?'

Justin didn't hesitate. 'Oh, Eddie Van Halen's one on "Beat it".'

'Not Slash's one on "Black or White"?' the DJ countered.

Justin's answer was curt and quintessentially English. 'Certainly not.'

It was a bit pathetic perhaps, but I felt patriotic, and desperately wanted them to go down well. If they could be successful in the US, perhaps this would spawn other similar like-minded bands. I was as loyal to my favourite bands as I was to my favourite football team. I suppose loyalty is a strong trait of mine – though that trait would be tested to the limit in the coming years.

After terrible traffic approaching downtown San Diego, we found a local bar near the venue and I ordered a couple of much-needed drinks. Dad went to the bathroom while I ordered. He was gone for quite a while.

When he eventually came back the expression on his face was different. More intense. There was a vague smell of smoke about him, which was more noticeable as California had already banned smoking in bars years ago, but it was not the smell of a spliff, which I had assumed was his drug of choice since I'd seen that huge bag of weed on his desk. I didn't know what it was.

While he was gone, I'd started a conversation with some other people who were also going to the gig and Dad now joined in. He was fine, except for the embarrassing knack he had of speaking to me as if I was a little boy in front of these strangers, to whom I was trying to look cool. And given we were all into The Darkness, this was a rare moment when I could've actually achieved that. But Dad was just being a dad. No matter how much trance he listened to and how much weed he smoked, he would always be an embarrassing parent. That's what parents are meant to be, isn't it?

At some point in the conversation one of the dudes we were talking to leant over to Dad and said in a stage whisper, 'What you on, bud?'

'Crystal meth,' Dad mumbled back, his eyebrows dancing mischievously over the top of his large glasses.

I had no idea then what the effects of crystal meth were. I had barely heard of it, though I knew it was some sort of class A drug. For all I know, I thought to myself, Dad just said *menthol crystals*, you know, to help him shift some stubborn catarrh he'd had lurking in his sinuses after a cold. Yes, that must have been it. Far more likely for him than some strong crack-like narcotic. Anyway, no time to dwell on that, it was show time.

The gig rocked, as expected. It was steamy, hot, packed, and very, very loud. In many ways, an old-school rock gig. Everyone seemed to love it. But despite the spectacle, I was keeping an eye on Dad. I was conscious of him continuously looking around, less interested in the actual band, but more in the people that were there, wide-eyed like a newborn baby. He'd never experienced anything like it, and whatever he was on would have just heightened the effect. There was something very camp about the whole thing, of course. The long-haired blokes in spandex gyrating around the stage with similar-looking characters in the audience. No wonder Dad was up for it!

He was definitely the oldest person there, as far as I could see. I saw a girl look at him at one point and smile, as if to say, 'Isn't that cute? Bringing the sweet old man to a rock concert!' I should've capitalised on that moment, explained to the girl how he didn't get out much so I was doing my best as a loving, caring son to get him into the community. Surely she'd want to shag me after hearing that? But of course, not only did I not have the balls to say anything to her, but I'd just started seeing this girl back in London, and unlike my Gaydar-trawling Dad, I liked the idea of monogamy. Hell, I was amazed I had a girlfriend at all, so I'd do nothing to jeopardise that.

After the gig, as Dad drove us back up Interstate 5, he was obviously struggling to stay awake. Coming down from whatever he'd been on all night, no doubt. He was shifting about in his seat, biting his lip, leaning forward to see the road better.

Eventually I said, 'Dad, if you're tired, I can drive.'

'No, no, it's OK. I'm fine.'

'Why not?' I said, suddenly feeling as if he was talking to me like a little kid again, like I didn't know how to drive a car. So I added boastfully, 'I've driven round the whole of the States. I can do it no problem.'

And I wasn't talking out of my arse. I really had. Well, not round the *whole* of the States exactly, but from Atlanta, Georgia to New Orleans in Louisiana. So that was about four states then.

It was back in 1996 after Jake had emigrated with his family to Atlanta. He had managed to get us volunteer places at the Olympic Games, which were being held there that year. We decided, with a lack of planning typical of us at the time, to drive to New Orleans for a short road trip before the Olympics began. We set out before dawn for some stupid reason, in Jake's Mum's car. Soon after we crossed into the state of Alabama, Jake said he was tired from driving, so I took over and carried on down the highway. I had no US driving licence at the time, but that was OK, wasn't it? I had a British one. British trumps American. After driving for a while, I decided to change the music. There was no conversation as Jake was asleep and I needed something to relieve the boredom. As I bent down to eject the cassette tape, the car veered to the left and hit a bumpy part of the road. In my (also) tired state, I panicked and overcorrected to the right which put the car in a spin. I then overcorrected back the other way, and put the car in an even more extreme spin, crossed the barrier between the two highways (thankfully there was no physical barrier, just a ditch), crossed the other highway with the oncoming traffic, thankfully missing any cars, and slid into the ditch at the side of the road.

Jake, not surprisingly, woke during our little pirouette across the interstate, screaming 'James! James!' I was glad he was trying to get the conversation going again but his timing was a bit off – I was otherwise engaged and couldn't enter into a dialogue right then. When the car eventually stopped, we sat there frozen in shock, but I remember the tape still playing as if nothing had happened and the Chili Peppers still singing (appropriately enough) about a rollercoaster. Luckily, there was not a scratch on either of us, just a few marks in our underwear perhaps.

Then Jake started shouting, 'Get out! It's going to blow!'

We threw ourselves at our respective doors. Jake, in his panicked state, tried to open his but failed because that side of the car was up against the side of the ditch. More panic as he climbed out my side and we ran from the car that was apparently about to explode just like in all those Hollywood films we'd seen.

Five minutes passed and we realised that, in fact, there wouldn't be as dramatic an ending as we'd expected, and we slowly filed back to the car. A cop soon turned up at the scene, told us we were lucky to be alive (he'd seen a similar crash recently in which everyone was killed), and that the sheriff would come and take our details shortly.

While we waited for him, a realisation hit us: I'd crashed a car in Alabama, I was British, and I had no driving licence. And I wasn't insured. Jake gallantly agreed to take the blame for the crash and tell the officer he was driving. So we swapped clothes, thinking that our appearance would already have been noted down and relayed back to the Police Department. No one would notice the swap, surely! However, Jake wore strong glasses, I didn't, so we were both struggling to see as we stood by the car, and the sheriff approached.

'Licence and registration please, boy.'

I waited for Jake to hand over his documents but he didn't move.

'Licence and registration please.'

I nudged Jake. Because I was wearing his glasses he had no idea the sheriff was even talking to him. But still he didn't move.

'You ignoring me?'

My head was beginning to ache now trying to see through Jake's thick lenses.

The sheriff put his face in mine so I couldn't fail to understand this time. 'Do you have some mental retardation? Licence and registration.'

'Oh. I'm sorry. I didn't realise you were talking to me, erm…'

As things became a little clearer for Jake too, he tried to come to my rescue, 'But I was driving, sir.'

The cop turned on Jake. 'Well, that's a whole crock of shit and you know it. I know it was your friend here driving.'

Oh God, we're doomed. We're going to be thrown in a cell. Probably share it with some of the characters from *Deliverance* or something.

Then the sheriff, added, 'But I'm gonna let you take the blame. 'Cause if we did record your British friend here as driving, he'd be spending the night in jail.'

'Oh, thank you, thank you, sir,' I said, handing Jake's glasses back to him and focusing on the genial face of our mercifully merciful patrolman.

So instead of being made to squeal like a pig by my cell mates, all I had to endure was a long, agonising drive back to Atlanta in a pick-up truck and the wrath of my best friend's mum when we got there.

With this little memory in mind, perhaps I wasn't the best person to take over from my dad right then on the way back to L.A. So when he barked, 'Please, James, just let me drive!' I stopped insisting and left him to get on with it.

Until his head dropped forward a few minutes later and he fell asleep at the wheel.

'DAAAAAD!' I shouted as loudly as I could – to try and inject some revitalising adrenaline into his veins; not because I was shitting myself, of course.

It seemed to do the trick and the rest of the drive was a lot less eventful than mine and Jake's to New Orleans.

We'd decided to treat ourselves to a luxury hotel in Beverly Hills that night, but far from raiding the mini bar and trying on the fluffy bathrobes and slippers, or marvelling at the marble washbasins in the en suite, I just wanted to collapse into my queen-size bed and get some rest after such an exhausting drive. Dad, I assumed, would do the same, although of course before jumping into his bed he'd probably make time to shovel all those free luxury toiletries into his suitcase, which were almost as good to him as a heavily discounted pack of Tesco Weetabix. However, as my head sank deeper and deeper into my downy pillows, instead of coming out the bathroom laden with freebies, my dad came out in a fresh tank top saying, 'James, I'm going to head out for a couple of hours, see what's going on. It's supposed to be a great place to go out at night round here.'

'Are you serious?' I groaned into a pillow. 'It's midnight, aren't you knackered? How long are you going to stay out? Where are you going to go?'

Oh. My. God. I sound like a parent, I thought to myself. I sound like Dad did, like Mum did when I was a teenager. *How long are you going to be? Where are you going?* I'm living that new film *Freaky Friday* where Jamie Lee Curtis swaps bodies with her daughter.

Dad smiled sheepishly. 'Just round here. I'll probably be back in the morning so please don't wait up for me, and don't worry, I'll be fine.'

'The morning? You'll be knackered,' I said with great authority, since I was already the knackered I spoke of. But of course I had no idea that the substance Dad was using could keep him up all night and stave off fatigue for hours and hours. I, however, was too tired to argue. So, resigned to the notion that my dad of course could not resist the opportunity to go and explore his sexuality in the gay epicentre of L.A., I mumbled into my duvet, 'OK, fine. Be safe. Be careful.' Yes, I said *that* to my *dad*.

I still to this day have no idea what he got up to that night and I'm not sure I want to know, but as the edges of the opulent curtains in our room glowed with the Californian sunrise I looked at my watch. Seven a.m. Still no sign of—

And then he crept into the room. I pretended to be asleep, lest he know that I was awake and worrying like the mother of a teenager, lest I start laying into him for worrying me. He visited the bathroom and I heard him humming a throbbing dance floor-filler that was obviously still ringing in his ears from whichever club he'd pogoed around last. Then he slipped into bed, let out a massively contented moan, which sounded far too much like a sound Sasithorn Sonjohnkoksoong once elicited from me, and began to snore. He spent the rest of the day in bed and I spent it sunning myself by the pool and contemplating what had happened to the middle-class, middle-aged, respected Jewish coin-dealing married man from suburbia that used to be my father.

CHAPTER 11
CRUISING

By the time we got to New York, the cruise was on both our minds – although for Dad, in hindsight, it may have been for very different reasons to me.

For me it was something new, exciting and a one-off – a bit of history that we would be part of. It was quite an event. At the time the *Queen Mary 2* was the largest and longest passenger ship ever built, and on her return to the UK after the maiden voyage to New York she would be accompanied by the *QE2* as a symbolic passing of the baton between the two ships. I never subscribed to that describing ships as female thing, but as the excitement grew, I couldn't help but enter into the spirit of it all.

First, however, we had to amuse ourselves for a few days in NYC before we set sail. So we spent time with more family we had there, did a bit of sightseeing and visited FAO Schwarz, the New York answer to Hamleys. When I was a boy a visit to FAO Schwarz would be the highlight of my trip over here. Now, of course, those days were long gone: the days of the Dickensian shop and the innocent coin dealer who proudly ran it, the days of the dad who'd take me to McDonald's and smile as my eyes lit up when presented with a large portion of fries. The dad I had now was way cooler in many ways (if you think lots of sex, drugs and rock 'n' roll – or happy house in this case – is cool, which of course I did), but standing there among the gigantic teddy bears in FAO Schwarz, I felt tiny again, and a sense of longing for my boring nine-to-five dad washed over me so strongly that it had me almost sucking my thumb and reaching for the nearest soft toy.

So a run was in order. Running had become a new hobby of mine, an opportunity to switch off, listen to music and stay fit at the same time. And during my travels, it was a great way to discover the environment and become a part of wherever I was. For that short jog I was just another resident, relieved of tourist status. I was also aware that being confined on a ship for seven days, no matter how big it may be, could prove to be a little suffocating, so I ran around Central Park, relishing the sense of freedom that came my way on the fresh, cold air of Manhattan.

The morning of the cruise arrived, and there was a palpable feeling of anticipation. As we approached the harbour in a taxi we saw the dramatic, imposing shape of the docked metal behemoth floating there. Dad and I exchanged suitable superlatives, jumped out of the taxi and took a selfie by the grand gangplank. We were off to a good start.

The *Queen Mary 2* seemed even more massive on the inside. Corridors went on forever, there were as many decks as a tall building has floors – eighteen in fact. She boasted fifteen restaurants and bars, five swimming pools, a casino, a ballroom, a theatre, and the first planetarium at sea – a joy for a sci-fi geek like me. Initial impressions surpassed expectations. Our room wasn't huge, but the balcony overlooked the side of the ship and we were on one of the upper decks. I leant out over it – the excited little boy in the toy shop again – and gulped at the giddy view from the top of a sheer wall of iron with the ocean lapping gently at the base far, far below. It felt impossible that the ship wouldn't keel over under its own weight. I straightened up quickly, a little vertigo coming over me, and looked around at Dad who was eagerly hanging up an array of tank tops in the cabin wardrobe. 'Nah! You're overthinking things as usual, James,' I said to myself.

'Let's go up on deck, Dad, and watch the departure!'

From the top deck we saw a huge flotilla to the left, right and behind the ship as we started to push off. There were fireworks, songs, and crowds of cheering people on the dock waving us off. Then, through the forest of grey hair and blue rinses of the OAPs around me, who seemed to make up a large proportion of the passengers on the cruise, I spotted the distinctive silver hair and beard of Terry Waite, who was still quite the celebrity back then, but unlike many others, he was famous for being thoroughly decent and a bit of a hero, and it made me feel even more that this was a special voyage on a special boat.

CRUISING

So the trip began. We spent a lot of time exploring the ship – that took a good couple of days. We spent a lot of time eating – there was unlimited food available 24/7; I'd never seen the blue rinses move so fast when it came to assaulting the buffet. Then I spent a lot of time trying to burn off all that food in the gym – although the pitch and roll of the ship made the treadmill more like a hike through the Alps. We spent time listening to lectures on astrophysics in the planetarium, given by experts who tried to explain to us laypeople the latest theoretical models on how our universe began... and how it would all end – cheery, I know! And it didn't really help the sense of impending doom that started to creep into my mind as the seas became a little rougher and I suddenly saw myself as a character in a disaster movie, images of Kate and Leo still fresh in my head from the most expensive movie ever made just a few years before. And to top it all, at the end of each day we were treated to the classic cruise liner show: all-singing, all-dancing and to compère, the one and only Des O'Connor. (Like I said, a disaster movie.)

Despite all this stimulation, there was still plenty of time to kill, so one day Dad and I found ourselves wandering into the casino. I'd done a little gambling by that time, and knew my way around a roulette table, to a certain extent – it all helped with my carefully cultivated, and massively deluded, self-image as James Bond. And if I was likely to be addicted to anything in my life, I reckon it would be gambling. Even though I was well aware it was a mug's game, I equally enjoyed that rush of adrenaline just before the ball dropped, the moment of possibility that I could double, triple, quadruple my money in a second with seemingly no work needed to achieve it. Dad had always liked a good return on his investments too, but his addictions, as it turned out, would lie in other areas. Nevertheless, I shepherded him over to a roulette table with a couple of spare seats and we sat down. I sat on one side of him and on the other side, I immediately noticed, was the leathery and rather orange TV personality Des O'Connor himself. A waitress quickly swooped over and asked us if we'd like a drink.

'Ooh, sparkling water, please,' Dad said.

'Martini, shaken, not stirred,' I said getting caught up in the moment.

The waitress looked at me like an impatient primary school teacher waiting for a sensible answer to an elementary question.

'I mean a vodka martini,' I stuttered. 'Please.' I flicked a look at Des O'Connor who was doing his best not to laugh, I think.

So cool, James, so cool!

Instead of scurrying back to my cabin red-faced, I decided to try and *style it out* – a phrase that I, of course, never have much use for – and started playing. Soon enough I started to get a few bets coming in. No major shakes, almost always a very moderate corner or split bet, certainly nothing to get excited about – unless you were my dad who would exclaim, loudly, 'Is that you!? Amazing! Well done, son!'

'All right, Dad, keep it down. No big deal,' I said, smiling uncomfortably at Des.

Another bet of mine came in and once again Dad jumped up and cried, 'I don't believe it, you've done it again! Clever boy!'

I winced with embarrassment, especially when I noticed that Des couldn't take his eyes off my dad now. Despite having interviewed some of the most colourful people in the world over his long career, Des O'Connor, Mr Entertainment himself, seemed fixated by the little Jew with the big glasses who was hopping about in his seat with joy at my little wins.

I just had to share with Dad the knowledge that we were playing roulette with a national treasure, if only to make him shut up and stop embarrassing me. So when Des was busy stacking up a particularly tall pile of chips on red 36, I whispered in Dad's ear, 'Before I tell you what I'm about to say, make sure you don't react, OK?'

Dad, loudly: 'What's that?'

Me, more slowly and determined: 'I said, before I tell you, don't react, OK?'

Dad, looking confused: 'OK.'

Me in hushed tones: 'Don't look now, but you're sitting next to Des O'Connor.'

Dad: 'Who?'

Me, becoming increasingly irritated: 'Shhh! Des O'Connor. You're sitting next to Des O'Connor.'

Dad, swivelling on his chair a hundred and eighty degrees: 'Where's Des O'Connor?' he blurted, looking straight at the perma-tanned presenter, who returned the stare, having already resumed his fascination with my father.

My cheeks burning, I fixed my stare back on the roulette table, pretending that hadn't just happened, my efforts to be James Bond at the casino in tatters. Now I knew exactly what my mum felt like all those years he drove her up the wall. After spending just half a week with my dad, sleeping in the same cabin, eating all our meals together, hanging out together every day, he had definitely started to grate. And he wasn't doing much to help the image I was trying desperately to project of a virile, heterosexual bachelor as I tried to realise my fantasy of a sexual encounter or two on this twenty-first-century Love Boat.

As we wandered round the vast liner we would meet various people, mainly because Dad, with all those social skills he used to exploit in his days at the shop, was very good at befriending strangers. I was less interested but maintained a polite disposition with each encounter. As well as the large proportion of elderly people on the ship, it soon dawned on me that the other major contingent here was gay men. This was rammed home, so to speak, with meetings such as the one with Peter from Switzerland, a very wealthy, mature-looking investment broker, and Bruno, his muscular, bored-looking toy boy.

'So, how are you enjoying the cruise?' Peter asked us cheerfully.

'Oh, it's wonderful, isn't it?' Dad said. 'I'd better stop eating though, otherwise they'll have to roll me off the ship.'

I cringed, since that was the eighth time he'd used that joke today.

Peter roared with laughter, however, and put a hand on Bruno's bulging bicep. 'Ha! He's so funny, isn't he?' Bruno seemed more worried about Peter's hand potentially creasing his Dolce and Gabbana shirt. Oblivious, Peter added, 'How long have you guys been together?'

The pause which followed was excruciating until I broke it with an awkward and mirthless laugh, 'No, no! He's my dad.'

'Yes, he's my son.'

'Oh sorry!' Peter said to me, unfazed. 'I thought you were his toy boy. How silly of me! Ironic really, since when we flew into New York last week the immigration officer thought Bruno and I were father and son.' He beamed. He clearly loved that, in a slightly incestuous way, which Freud would no doubt have had a field day with.

Bruno rolled his eyes at me; clearly he didn't love it as much as Peter. I, however, was busy quietly fuming at the idea that anyone could think I was Dad's toy boy. If I was gay, I ranted inwardly, I would be way out his league.

Then Bruno winked at me, and rather than being flattered and taking it as corroboration of my inner rant, I despaired of my chances of ever realising that fantasy of mine out here on the high seas. And although Bruno had a body I could only dream about for myself as I staggered about in the ship's gyrating gym, I didn't want to be seen as him – some brainless, blonde arm-candy for a sugar daddy… and for *my* daddy at that! It was weird, unpalatable and downright bizarre to me. But it started to make sense to me now why Dad had booked this cruise in the first place. Like Limehouse, where his new flat was, like West Hollywood where he'd booked our hotel in L.A., cruise ships were hotbeds of gay activity, and, like a freed prisoner running over open countryside, he wanted to be in the thick of it. And, once I felt I had advertised it enough on every deck that I was most definitely hetero, I was actually glad of the gay contingent on the ship – the old people spent most of their time moaning about anything they could find to complain about, while the homosexuals seemed to revel in the cheesiness of the experience; always happy, cheerful, up for a laugh and… well, gay.

Nevertheless, Dad and I started to spend more and more time apart as the cruise wore on. He was cramping my style! A thought that was validated one night when, whilst walking, sans Dad, through the 'town centre' of the ship, as it was known, I heard the rare sound of a female voice saying, 'Hiya!' in my direction. So rare it was that I almost carried on walking, knowing it couldn't possibly be aimed at me, but something – my desperately aching balls, perhaps – told me to look up. And there was one of the dancers from Des O'Connor's nightly show waving at me.

'Me? Is she actually looking at me?' I thought incredulously. I refused to believe it until I'd walked so close to her that I could see her eyes were not fixed over my shoulder at some hetero Bruno lookalike posing there. 'She must be lost or something. Probably thinks I'm a member of the crew who can help her. Or perhaps she just wants change for the fruit machines. Or someone to carry her bags and I look like the bloody bellboy.' Whatever it was, I told myself to play it cool, so I stood there as she approached, epileptically trying to find something to do with my hands in the most uncool way ever.

I remembered her well, because the other night Dad and I had been sitting very close to one side of the stage during the show, and she'd been dancing on our side. At one moment we'd made eye contact. I remembered wondering whether that meant anything at all; it was longer than it needed to be. At the time I'd quickly dismissed it and moved on – like I had a choice! But perhaps it did mean something, and perhaps this fantasy sexual encounter was about to be turned into a reality at long bloody last.

We began to chat, and incredibly it seemed she didn't want directions, change, or someone to carry a suitcase – it really was a let's-get-to-know-each-other conversation. She even invited me to come with her to the ship's nightclub, G32. Hoping that the G didn't stand for Gay and that she wasn't a lesbian, I nearly bit her arm off. Trying desperately to maintain my composure I followed her, spaniel-like, to the club. As soon as we got inside, she noticed more of her dance troupe sitting round a table. They waved her over and she hurried into their midst. I waited for her to beckon me over too, far too chicken to invite myself to sit down.

No invitation came, as she was immediately engrossed in a conversation. There was room for one more at the table, I deduced; room for a little one, anyway. And just as I had gathered up the courage to march over and plonk myself next to her hard enough to jolt her from her chat and remind her of this catch she'd met outside, Des O'fucking Connor turned up and positioned himself right in the middle of all the girls, right in that space that was meant for me. All the girls, my 'date' included, proceeded to fawn over him. And I turned, shoulders drooped, cock-blocked by an orange, wrinkly seventy-something.

So I resigned myself to a drink at the bar and began to, er, people watch – just like another night at the Fire Station at Bournemouth University.

Des was the life and soul of the party. He was the oldest guy in the club, but looked like he had more energy than anyone else. It was 2 a.m. in the morning, and even when he danced it wasn't the dad dance you'd expect. Everyone loved him. And he knew it.

I hated him.

I slipped out of the club soon after and, just to rub it in, I saw Dad slipping into a cabin – and it wasn't ours.

Those last few days, I was almost desperate to see landfall. It sounds unappreciative now, but as we approached the dreary, grey, drizzly docks of Southampton, observed by a few bedraggled onlookers at most, I remembered the excitement and buzz of the flotilla and fireworks in NYC and I thought, 'How fucking apt!'

CHAPTER 12

TROMBONING

'Right, are you all sitting comfortably?' Dad was excited.

I sighed. 'Yes, Dad.'

'Just get on with it, Richard, for God's sake!' Mum grumbled. 'I don't have all day, you know.'

'OK, here we go!' He pressed play on the camcorder and hurried to the sofa, eager not to miss a moment of our holiday video.

Nothing happened. The screen remained blank.

'Very dark on the *Queen Mary*, was it?' Mum smirked.

Dad swore and scampered back to the camcorder, fiddling with the wires that connected it – or perhaps not in this case – to the TV. 'Is your TV broken, Marilyn?'

'Oh yes, it must be my TV, mustn't it. Couldn't possibly be the fact you have no idea how to use it, let alone that stupid camera thing.'

I smiled. It was just like old times.

'Let me look, Dad.' I sprang up out of my seat, but Dad blocked me from the camcorder with his arse. Since it, like the rest of his body, was a lot skinnier than it used to be, it proved to be no great obstacle, but I let him feel like he was in control and just said over his shoulder that he might try turning the TV onto auxiliary mode.

'Mum, where's the remote?'

'Here, darling,' she said, picking it up off the arm of the chair in which she sat.

I took the remote and flicked to the AUX setting. Immediately images of the *Queen Mary 2*, resplendent in the dock in New York City, came glowing into the room.

'See! I knew it was the TV that was the problem,' Dad said. 'Oh, now we've missed half of it.'

'We've missed thirty seconds, Dad,' I said. 'Come and sit down!'

But he was fiddling with the camcorder again.

'A bad workman always blames his tools,' Mum muttered.

He was rewinding right to the very beginning lest we miss the first few minutes of the *Queen Mary 2* in dock, which resembled very closely the next few minutes of the *Queen Mary 2* in dock. Jeez! We might as well have been looking at a photograph. It was hardly Spielberg.

Finally Dad sat that newly skinny arse of his back on the sofa and I couldn't help but grin to myself as I looked at us three sitting there as a family watching boring home videos that go on for hours and hours – just like normal families do. Of course, we were sitting in the opulent surroundings of my mother's lover's flat as we did this normal stuff, but that was just a minor detail. And I was quite happy that we were able to do it here in Ruth's place. She was at work now, but totally cool with Dad and Mum still meeting up on occasions like this – I suppose she was hardly threatened, sexually speaking, by my gay dad. In fact Ruth and Dad got on very well.

And so I relived that bizarre, amazing, annoying and claustrophobic seven-day cruise again through the tromboning and shaky lens of my father's camcorder, which it seemed he never let go of throughout the voyage. Or rather, I saw for the first time loads of random people he had met and with whom he had seemingly struck up a close relationship within a matter of days. For example, there was an older lady, who shone out from underneath a cloud of white hair, professing her love for him, saying to the camera how wonderful it was to meet him and how much she would miss him when the cruise was over. Nearly all these people were strangers to me; I had never met them myself. It seemed, whilst I was failing to be James Bond in the casino or getting socially gazumped by Des O'Connor, Dad had been off wandering around the ship, doing what he's good at: meeting people and striking up an immediate rapport with them. I was partly envious, partly in awe. But mostly just bored out of my mind, until a shot of Peter the investment banker, laughing and raising his glass of champagne to the camera as he sat at a table in one of the numerous bars, cut abruptly to a shot of Peter the investment banker completely starkers on his knees in the half light of a cabin, his face rammed between the gym-firm buttocks of Bruno who stood before him. My father was still, presumably, the cameraman, the shot more shaky than ever, but the only tromboning going on now, it seemed, was on Bruno's rather impressive instrument.

Dad dived for the camcorder. I dived for the remote. Mum rolled her eyes and went to the kitchen.

'I don't know what that was all about,' Dad called after her. 'Must have been what someone had recorded on there before me.'

I tutted and huffed to let my dad know how disappointed I was in him and followed Mum to the kitchen, where I found her knocking her head back, hand clamped to her mouth.

'Sorry you had to see that, Mum.'

She washed down whatever she'd just taken with a glass of water.

'Shame he turned it off,' she scoffed. 'It was finally getting interesting.'

'Are you OK?' I said, suddenly overcome with the notion that she had started doing drugs too, as she slipped a box of pills back into a drawer.

'I'm fine. Just paracetamol,' she said, noting the paranoia in my voice. 'Your father gives me a headache. You know that.'

*

'A rusty trombone.'

'A what?'

'A rusty trombone,' Will said, clapping his hands with glee and throwing himself back into the sofa. 'That's what that invest-ment banker was doing to his toy boy. That's what they call it.'

'You mean it's actually a thing? Like, it has a name?' I grimaced, drawing long and hard on a joint before passing it to Jake, who shook his Jewfro at me, too absorbed in shooting up zombies on the PlayStation to even have a toke.

But not too absorbed to ask Will, 'How do *you* know?'

'How do I know what?' Will said.

'How do you know it's called a rusty trombone?'

Will blushed and grabbed the spliff.

CHAPTER 13

DATING DAVROS?

The girl I'd been seeing before the cruise had – how did she put it? – decided to keep her options open. How did I put it? She dumped me. It was no great surprise to me and probably is not to you, dear reader, since by now you probably have a fair grasp of my prowess in the dating field: akin to the average rugby player's facility for ballet, blindfolded. Nevertheless, I was undeterred and looked again at the site Jake said was the source of his greatest conquests – Jdate.com.

'Your resource for all things Jewish dating,' I read from the website's homepage.

'Some tasty chicks on there, mate,' Jake said as he drained a can of Stella and slid the rest of the Pizza Hut Hawaiian across the sofa at me. 'Taking one out for dinner now, in fact.'

'But you've just had pizza!' I said, beginning to devour his decidedly unkosher takeaway.

'Yeah, but you know these fancy restaurants. I'll probably come out starving at the end if I don't have something decent to eat beforehand.'

I started scrolling through the Jdate site. 'How the bloody hell do any of these girls go for you?' I called out as Jake slipped his trainers on and wiped the pizza sauce from his jeans with the dishcloth.

'How do I look?'

'Like the lovechild of Worzel Gummidge and Gene Wilder.'

'It's the hair,' Jake grinned.

'What?' I said, stuffing my face with another slice of ham and pineapple and reading an article on the website about how to survive Passover as a singleton.

'The Jewfro. It gets their attention. It's my USP. You've got to have a USP.' And he bounced out of the flat.

Jake had a point. As a marketing professional now, the idea appealed to me. But what was my USP?

Erm.

Erm.

Ooh, I know! I bet I would be the only Jew these girls had ever met with two gay parents and a middle-aged father who does pills and loves raving and S&M orgies. Hmm, but that probably wouldn't go down too well on a first date. Or a second, if I ever got that far. OK, we can work on the USP, I told myself as I signed up to Jdate and tried to apply some other facets of my professional knowledge to marketing myself.

And if I knew anything about advertising, it was about creating a winning visual brand identity. How do you stand apart from your competitors? How do you tell a story without saying a word? As far as dating websites go, this is all in your photographs, of course. So for a few smoke-filled, pizza-munching hours I agonised over which photos to put on my profile and what they said about me. One of me smouldering against the New York skyline told prospective dates I was well-travelled and unfazed by the glitz and glamour of the metropolis, while another of me laughing against a backdrop of foliage told them I was fun to be around, natural and unpretentious. My arm began to ache under the strain of all the selfies I took: if the lighting was flattering then the pose was wrong; if the pose was cool, the lighting showed the dark circles under my eyes. I thought of Dad and his unselfies and suddenly had a sinking feeling that I might still be doing this when I was his age.

As well as getting your own photo right, the second rule of internet dating is: never ever go for a profile with just one photo on it. You know how long you spent getting your photos just right and you know, deep down anyway, how they're the best possible (sometimes unrealistic) looking version of you. So when you notice the girl of your dreams among all the other profile pictures scrolling before you like a human fruit machine, be disciplined! Ask yourself why, out of the multitude of photos that beauty would have to offer, she could only put forward one. You may think I'm being cold and callous, but it's no revelation to say that, for the male at least, attraction needs to be physical too. I'm just trying to save you all a lot of time and heartache here, people, because this is a question I didn't ask myself until it was too late.

The third rule of internet dating is: translate the profile text. Mature means old. Fiery means psychotic. Great personality means minging. Loyal means stalker. Likes the finer things in life means gold-digger. Curvy means grossly overweight. Bubbly means grossly overweight and annoying. My profile read:

Modern man [we'll be splitting the bill 50/50 'cause I can't afford all these dates], *told I'm attractive* [by my mum] *not just looking for sex* [cunning reverse psychology there], *not into email tennis* [need to get an actual date ASAP before you suss out what a geek I am].

Needless to say, when the tidal wave of enquiries expected turned out to be the dripping of a tightly closed faucet, I was reduced to opening emails from a girl who didn't even have one photo of herself on her profile, which of course translates as: best dated with a paper bag on her head. But, I told myself, she might be a master of marketing herself and the no-photo thing was actually a means of making an enigma of herself, drawing me in, clickbait, no less.

And I clicked. But I was no fool. My first message asked for photos. Politely demanded photos in fact. I had no doubt that she would then run a virtual mile back into the dark and anonymous ether from which she had emerged, or that I would be the one dashing through cyberspace in an effort to escape the monster she clearly – The photos arrived promptly – wasn't.

She was an attractive – no, really attractive, not attractive in internet speak, where attractive means plain – redheaded, blue-eyed, petite-looking twenty-year-old (five years my junior), called Vicki. We swapped numbers, spoke on the phone – me doing my best Roger Moore impression throughout, which was bound to impress her – and arranged to meet in a Middle Eastern shisha bar not far from the flat in Clapham. She lived just down the road in Tooting, which was a bonus, since nearly every other Jewish girl in the world seemed to live far north of the river in Barnet.

When the big night came, I sat in the bar nervously waiting for her to arrive, trying out various poses on the low-slung couches the bar was furnished with, wondering if this red lighting brought my zits out more or just homogenised all the blemishes into a smooth-looking scarlet. My nerves, however, were not so much for my posture and complexion, but for whether Vicki, given she had only sent photos of herself from the waist up, was going to trundle in on a Dalek's lower half, like a female Davros. Clearly I had been watching too many *Dr Who* reruns in the run up to the revival of the classic sci-fi series, which was about to begin again on the BBC this very month with Christopher Eccleston as the ninth incarnation of the Doctor. I wondered if I should share my excitement about this with Vicki until I heard Jake's voice in my head shouting, 'Don't be a dick!'

And suddenly there she was, looking even better than her photos – or perhaps that was just my relief at her having both legs intact as opposed to a locomotive cyborg base.

After an awkward greeting where I shook her hand rather than giving her a European-style kiss on both cheeks, which would have made her feel like she was in the presence of a confident cosmopolitan gent instead of a candidate interviewing for a job, I asked, 'What can I get you to drink?'

Her response was devastating. 'Tea please.'

'Tea?'

'I know,' she giggled. 'Not very cool to ask for that at the bar, is it?'

No, but that wasn't the biggest problem I had with her choice of beverage. Without alcohol sloshing about inside her, as it would soon be inside me, how was I to convince her that I wasn't a complete bellend?

I ordered the tea nevertheless and hovered over the wine list, considering taking it back to Vicki to show her all the fruity vintages she could choose from before fast-forwarding in my mind to the moment she told me to stop pressuring her to drink and the meathead sitting on the couch next to ours chivalrously intervened and beat me shitless. I doubted that would result in a second date so headed back over to her, the teacup rattling against its saucer and betraying my trembling hand.

Despite her lack of intoxication and my increasing level of it, we got on well. She was giggly, flirty even, all the signs were good. I daydreamed of going in for the kiss on various occasions, but still couldn't muster the necessary kahooners, fearing they'd be kicked in if I did. I went back to the bar for another round of beer and tea and as I returned to the couch I noticed that the aforementioned meathead was not only playing a part in my imagined future but in my actual bloody present too. He'd had the audacity to lean over from his couch and start chatting to Vicki. And what was worse, she appeared to be enjoying it. Part of me wanted to take him aside and give him a damn good thrashing, and another (the real) part of me wanted to take him aside and beg him to tell me the secret of starting up a conversation like that with a girl in a bar.

Suddenly I was back on the Queen Bloody Mary watching Des O'-No-You-Didn't-Connor cockblocking me and I wasn't about to let it happen all over again. Any doubts I'd had about Vicki being girlfriend material, which to be honest were very few – after all, she had a pulse – were obliterated by the fact that she was clearly desirable to the kind of blokes I aspired to be, physically if not mentally. And so when I'd finally reached the couch, looking like Mrs Overall in my efforts not to spill the tea, I made my move. I swooped in with fish-like mouth. She was caught unawares, which was probably the only way I was likely to catch her, but surprisingly and thankfully, as far as my battered self-esteem was concerned, she went with it and in seconds we were in full snog mode. It was great. Twelve-pound-a-month subscription to Jdate well spent!

CHAPTER 14

MAN UP

My office phone rang.

'Hi, darling.'

'Hi, Mum. You OK?'

'Yes fine. It's been a while. You haven't called me for a couple of weeks.'

'I know, sorry. Just been so busy with work.' I wasn't lying. I really had been. I certainly wasn't avoiding her since that nonsense with Dad's camcorder. If I was avoiding anyone it was him.

'OK, well don't forget about your old Mum… OK?'

'Of course I won't.'

The line went so quiet I'd thought she'd hung up.

'Hello? Hel—'

'James, I want to come over to your flat with Ruth, I have something I want to tell you.'

The flat in question, by the way, was not the flat I used to share with Jake and Will. Well, now I had a girlfriend – yes, Vicki actually stuck with me after that first night, even though she was only on tea – I thought I should grow up and get my own place too, before she came round and saw the shithole I lived in with the boys and walked right out again. Yes, it was time to man up and strike out on my own, leave that childish bachelor pad behind and rent my very own flat… bought by my dad. Well, one step at a time, eh?

'I have something I want to tell you,' Mum repeated.

'Oh. Right. OK.' An email from a client popped up on the screen in front of me and distracted me slightly from the sense of déjà vu lapping at the edge of my senses. 'Can you not just tell me now?'

'No, James, I'd rather tell you face-to-face.'

I was a little thrown. I also felt a slight sense of irritation. I mean, why did she have to make a drama out of whatever the news was? I thought, 'Get over yourself, Mum! I can take it, I'm sure it's not that big a deal. You *and Dad* have done the whole coming out of the closet thing already – nothing can trump that.' With her making it a bigger deal than it needed to be, I was now starting to worry too, which was a bit selfish of her, I told myself.

Another email popped up.

'Come on, Mum, I'm not in the mood for games. Please, what is it about? At least give me a clue. Can you not give me a clue?'

'Please, James, just let me come over.'

'OK, Mum, fine.'

I made a hasty arrangement with her and hung up, leaving me with a week to stew over what this development could possibly be. I think it was fair to say I'd already had my fair share of parental bombshells. I recalled the anxious anticipation that preceded the meal with Dad at La Bonne Heure, as well as the meal two weeks later with Mum at The Gay Hussar. Now that feeling was upon me yet again.

I called Dad. It took him forever to answer the phone. When he finally did he greeted me with a lungful of phlegm. 'Oh, excuse me, James.' He coughed violently again. 'How are you?'

'I'm OK, Dad. I was just wondering if you knew what Mum was on about.'

'What do you mean?'

'I mean, what's so important she can't tell me over the phone.'

Dad coughed again so horrifically I asked him if he was OK.

'Oh yes, yes, fine thanks, James. But I must, erm, get back to… it.'

I could tell he knew about Mum's news already, but he was giving nothing away – Mum's orders, no doubt. And I had no desire to find out what exactly he had to get back to, so I hung up and spent the evening speculating with Vicki over what this news could be as she speculated over who would be doing the American Smooth and how many sequins would be worn on *Strictly Come Dancing.*

'Perhaps they're going to adopt a child. Can you even do that? I mean, if you're gay. I suppose you can nowadays.' I chewed this over with a mouthful of Doritos.

Vicki replied, 'I don't think Alesha Dixon should be allowed on this show. I mean she's a dancer already in a way, being from Mis-Teeq. The others don't stand a chance.'

'I wouldn't mind though. I quite like the idea of having a little brother or sister.'

'Oh my gosh, will someone put Willie Thorne out of his misery, he dances like a duck.'

I sat up. 'I know what it is. Ruth's got a villa in Vermont. I bet they've decided to go and live there together.' I slumped back into the sofa again. While I knew I'd be sad to see them go, I was happy for them. 'As long as it makes Mum happy, I can live with that.'

'What is he famous for, anyway? Never heard of him before now.'

'Snooker,' I grumbled as another thought nagged at me despite my conclusion. If they were just moving to America why was Mum so insistent that Vicki be there with me when she came over? Was that really necessary? Was she being over-dramatic again – a typical Jewish mother being overly protective of her little soldier?

So by the time I answered the door to Mum and Ruth a few days later, I was concerned again, anxious even; the anticipation was overpowering.

Mum was carrying a bottle of red wine, which she handed to me. Not her usual offering. That's odd, I thought.

'Thanks. What's this for?'

'Oh, I thought you might… like it, that's all.'

Curiouser and curiouser, I thought, trying to amuse myself. Little did I know how, just like Alice in Wonderland, my sense of reality was about to be distorted and stretched beyond my imagination.

The moment I knew something momentous, and not good momentous, was about to be revealed was when Ruth calmly beckoned Vicki over to her and said they were going for a 'little walk' outside. I exchanged a worried glance with her. It was as if she was being led out to be lynched in the alleyways of Kings Cross. Poor Vicki, this was all just as disorientating for her as it was for me.

I tried to stay calm as Mum sat me down and took my hand, a confirmation that this was going to hit me hard. I braced myself.

'Darling, you might remember I had to see the GP recently as my hip was hurting.'

I recalled the pills she took when Dad was over with the bloody camcorder. The ones she said were just for a headache.

'Yes?'

'Well, she thought it was a bit odd, so I had some more tests.'

I couldn't bear it any longer. I feared the worst and wanted the news straight up. 'Is it cancer?' I blurted out.

'Yes.'

There was a pause. A mighty pause. But none of your Pinteresque stuff. This wasn't a piece of theatre. This was fucking real. I was in shock, but bizarrely relieved after all the anticipation; at least now I knew. But the next question was, of course, how bad?

She spoke deliberately, softly, measuredly. As comforting a voice as she could possibly offer, bless her, even though it was her who needed comforting.

She went on, 'It's been diagnosed as ovarian cancer, but it's spread and that's why my hip hurts. Because it's had time to spread, or metastasise, as they say.' She smiled weakly, trying to soften the blow. She swallowed. She took a deep breath, as she must have done every time she had to say these words out loud or even just in her own head. 'They've told me it's terminal.'

That was it, the punch that sent me reeling. I tried to speak, but my voice was quivering so much, all I could get out was, 'How. Long?'

'If I have immediate surgery, which I will, I'll go private, I could have two and a half years. But it's difficult to say right now.'

I had nothing left to say.

So she carried on, 'I'm so sorry, James, I won't be able to see your children.' Now her attempts to keep it together started failing. 'I would have given the world for that, but it's probably not meant to be.'

Suddenly my hopelessness with girls took on a whole new urgency. I had an insane impulse to go and find Vicki and get her pregnant immediately, just so Mum could see the grandchildren she dreamt of. But her words suggested she suspected already, as I did deep down, no matter how much Mum and I wanted it, that Vicki wasn't going to be the mother of my children.

We continued to talk, but the rest was a haze, as I tried to comprehend the news. I asked about second opinions, the schedule of treatments, how Dad took it, but all the while my mind was swimming: I couldn't quite believe this moment was taking place. Mum was young, only fifty-eight, and she seemed perfectly healthy, fitter than she'd been for a while, ironically. I thought people with cancer looked ill. I was obviously wrong. Then before I knew it, the front door opened. Vicki and Ruth were back.

One of the most distinct memories I have of that evening is of Vicki's face when she came back into the flat – wracked with concern, searching my face to see how I'd taken the news that Ruth had imparted to her outside. It drove home how big, how life-changing this news was – it wasn't me overreacting here.

Ruth's soft, East Coast accent was comforting to me. 'Hey. Are you both OK?'

'Yes thanks,' we both mumbled.

After a few more hot-faced pauses and failed attempts at levity, it was time for Mum and Ruth to leave. I actually wanted them to go because I couldn't hold it together for much longer and I didn't want Mum to see me fall apart in front of her, at least not right now. It would have been hard enough for her just telling me the terrible news; I didn't want to make it worse.

I looked at the bottle of Cabernet on the kitchen counter. 'So why the wine, Mum?'

She smiled sadly. 'I thought you might need that after we go.'

Vicki and I ushered them out the door and, as soon as it shut, I allowed myself to break down on her. I hadn't cried for years, not since I'd been at school, because crying is for babies, right? It was a strange sensation after all this time. I'd forgotten how cathartic it could be and how exhausting the expression of deep emotions is.

The wine tasted good, but it wasn't strong enough to numb the pain. Nor was the morning after any brighter. If anything, remembering the night before was like reliving a nightmare. On reflection, there was of course no easy way for Mum to break that news, and I was grateful in the end to my Mum for insisting on Vicki being there with me. That shoulder to cry on was an important one to have, though Vicki's shoulders, like mine, felt far too young to be dealing with this shit.

CHAPTER 15

DEALING

I went to see Dad. Went to see how he'd taken the news of Mum's illness. I mean, despite their being separated, or rather because of it, they were getting on better than ever. He must have been devastated. However, when I arrived I was slightly miffed that it appeared to be business as usual for the coin dealer. In fact business seemed to be booming.

'I'll be right out, son. Make yourself comfortable,' Dad said as he disappeared into his office.

Make myself comfortable? How was I supposed to do that when the large L-shaped, expensive-looking sofa that now adorned the living room was littered with men I had never met? I was never the most confident in social situations and, despite my father's wish for me to take over the business, I still knew nothing about antique coins either, so what was I supposed to talk to them about?

One of the men waiting there took the lead and said, 'So you're Richard's son?' He held out his hand.

'Oh, yes. James. Pleased to meet you,' I said, shaking his hand and perching on the edge of the space he'd made for me next to him.

'Brian,' he said.

One of the other men followed suit and leant across to shake hands. 'Bayo,' he said in a deep West African accent.

'James,' I said again, rather pointlessly.

I looked at the third man, expecting him to introduce himself, but he seemed to be miles away so I didn't force the issue. Then there was a bit of a pause followed by, 'Your Dad's a bit of a character, isn't he?' Brian grinned.

'You could say that, yes. How long have you known him?' I asked, genuinely curious.

'Oh, for quite a while now.' Brian looked at Bayo, who concurred and smiled warmly at me. 'He always has the best quality stuff. He's really trustworthy. Such a great guy.'

'Yes, he's always very straight down the line when it comes to business.'

I always remembered with pride how Dad was regarded as one of the most straightforward, most trustworthy and honest people in the coin business, which was often pockmarked with dodgy dealings, shady characters and low-level corruption. This had been mentioned to me multiple times by a number of Dad's business colleagues and made me beam every time, as it did now.

There was another awkward pause in which Bayo continued to smile at me in a way that was more than warm and stroked his denim-clad inner thigh, much to my alarm.

'So,' Brian said, his voice now full of curiosity. 'You're OK with all this? I mean, it must be strange for you.'

What did he mean by that? I felt a brief lurch in my stomach; the kind that you get when you realise you've been kept in the dark about something; the kind that makes you feel isolated, helpless, and a sensation of panic began to bubble up inside me. The sight of another bloke popping his head out of the infamous second bedroom and beckoning Bayo in did nothing to quell my unease.

So that was it! That was what Brian was on about: there was another orgy going on in there. And while Dad was doing business in the office too! Was he nuts? What would his clients think? Were Brian and the other chap here to deal coins or were they, like Bayo, queuing for a go in the swing like kids at an X-rated theme park? Or both?

Luckily I couldn't answer Brian right then as the office door opened and a wraith of a bloke staggered out followed by my father. 'Brian?' he said.

Brian jumped up. So did I, in order to give Dad the most detailed quizzical look I could muster, which was so full of questions and eye pointing that he must have thought I was either having a seizure or just trying to masticate a particularly chewy toffee. Dad took nothing meaningful from my facial contortions and instead showed the wraith out of the flat and followed Brian into the office. In the process I had a good view through into the room: lights on, blinds down, despite the early hour of the day. And there on the desk next to the computer was what I can only describe as a host of drugs paraphernalia: glass pipes, high-end lighters, bags of pills and white powder and, as ever, his trusty weighing scales which now took on a whole new function.

'Won't be a sec.' Dad smiled at me and shut the door.

The sadomasochistic moans coming from the second bedroom suddenly paled into insignificance. I found I had all the grace and balance of a newborn foal, so I flopped back onto the sofa and sat staring at a replay in my head of the inside of Dad's office accompanied by those bloody alarm bells, which had sloughed off their mufflers and seemed to be played now by a thousand smug campanologists to the tune of *You Idiot, James. You Could Have Stopped This Back When You Saw That Bag Of Weed But Instead You Just Smoked Half Of It*. My head-in-the-sand decision had come back to bite me in the arse – an action which had just been carried out in the other room judging by the squeal that ricocheted down the corridor. I felt sick, weak, but most of all angry.

No wonder Diane had never come back. She was not only shocked by the sex show going on next to her work space, but she was now surplus to requirements, unless she wanted to keep accounts for Dad's drug-dealing business, which he probably didn't want documented with Di's usual diligence.

Drug dealing?

My dad, a drug dealer!

If I told Jake and Will about any more of these family bombshells they'd start to doubt my honesty. They'd think I was making stuff up just to get attention or something. Actually, in this case, they'd probably be over the moon because we'd no longer have to go to Alfie the Bear to get the goods: it was right here in our laps.

Oh my God! What was I even thinking that for?

I thought I might cry, and perhaps I would have if there hadn't been that other bloke lolling on the sofa. Thank God he wasn't the talkative type, as I couldn't have held a conversation right then. I was on the edge of freaking out, and I never freak out. Right, James, keep it together, stay calm, think! There could still be some other plausible explanation, I thought. Clutching at straws, yes, but what the fuck was there to lose? I had one final clutch. My dad is not a dealer. He's probably experimenting with drugs, just as he has been with his sex life, hence the stuff on his desk, but he is not a drug dealer. He is a coin dealer and these men are buying and selling coins. But, hang on, do they not have a problem with class A narcotics being strewn all over their business associate's desk as they try to get on with their numismatics? Clearly not. Because, you dufus, they are not here to numismat— whatever the verb is. They're here to buy drugs. Brian wasn't talking about the orgy when he said, 'You're OK with all this?' Or not just about the orgy anyway. He was talking about the drug dealing too.

I waited for Brian to come out of the office and bid his goodbyes, then I said, 'Dad, can I have a word?'

Dad raised his finger. 'One second, son, then I'm all yours. Ed?'

The guy on the sofa gurgled something and prised himself up. He too went into Dad's office and I was left waiting again. No Diane to amuse me like old times. No maternal knee to bounce up and down on, no carbon copy paper to draw on. No prospect of a trip to Hamleys after waiting for Dad to finish 'business' today. I felt simultaneously more childish and more grown up than ever: with a child-like sense of rejection I pouted while the grown-ups were talking, and with all the neurosis and anxious vigilance of a parent I waited to interrogate and scold the big kid in there who was going off the rails.

As I stewed, it occurred to me how everything was shifting. At the outset of Dad's new life, it was all fun and games and golden anecdotes to share with my mates or with girls I was trying to impress. At parties I was the raconteur for once, regaling people with funny, charming, edgy but entirely acceptable stories of life with my 'crazy' dad. And they lapped it up, as much as I enjoyed sharing. But fast forward to this moment and none of it felt funny or charming anymore. And I had no interest in sharing this latest revelation with anyone. The party was over, and I was left to deal with the consequences of one that had careered wildly out of control and was heading into territory I did not want to explore. Or, in other words: I was scared shitless. I got a glass of water to cool down, but as I drank, an image of Mum refracted in the bottom of the glass and I was fuming again. Dad was aware of her news too. How could he go on like nothing was happening?

Ed finally left the flat and I barged into the office and sat down in front of the smorgasbord of drugs on the desk. The filing cabinets were still there with the books on numismatics on top, but they looked like they hadn't been touched in weeks, perhaps months. I examined the windows, which I thought had had blinds on them, but there were no curtains or blinds on any window in this flat – high up on the seventeenth floor, I suppose they weren't necessary. Unless you were dealing drugs in one room. In which case you might, as Dad had done here, Sellotape black bin liners to the windows in a pretty half-hearted attempt, it must be said, to conceal his illegal activities. I could still see icons of the London skyline peeking through the considerable gaps between bin bags, and if I could see them, who could see us, I wondered, suddenly overcome with a sense of paranoia. I shifted in my seat to try and put one of those bin bags between me and the windows of a skyscraper. Bin bags, I scoffed. How appropriate for such a sullied little room.

'Hey, James,' Dad said, coming back into the room, 'Shall we go in the lounge?'

'Er, no, Dad. Let's sit right here and talk about all this.'

Dad hesitated at the door for a moment before conceding – there was no point in pretending anymore. He took his seat at the desk and tried to tidy some things away, as if I hadn't notice the huge bag of white powder and the scorched crack pipes yet.

'What's going on, Dad?'

'Oh… finished work for today… time to relax, eh?'

'I mean, what is all this? What happened to the coins? Is this your business now?'

'Oh, no, not really.'

Not really. I loathe that phrase. So wishy-washy. Surely either something is or it isn't. Nine times out of ten *no, not really* just means yes.

But Dad continued to bullshit. 'I just got a great deal on this stuff so I was giving some out to friends.'

I recalled that that was exactly what he'd said about the big bag of weed on his desk a few years back. I knew my dad was generous, but he was also shrewd with money. I doubted he would have been giving away stuff with such a large street value.

'Do you give it to them? Or do they pay for it?'

'Well, they pay, but only face value.'

That was the nugget of information I was waiting for. 'Dad!' I exploded, 'You're a drug dealer!'

'No, don't be silly.'

'Don't be silly?' I said with contempt. 'I'm not the one being silly. You are. In fact, you're being completely insane.'

Dad tutted, got up and closed the office door, lest my ranting disturb the orgy down the corridor, God forbid!

'How can you do this?' I said. 'Is it really worth being arrested for? Going to prison for? You're taking a massive risk, Dad.'

'No, no, I'm not going to be arrested, James. I'm small fry. The police aren't interested in a small-time deal— I mean, someone like me. Besides I'm only dea— *supplying* my friends, just a small group of people that I know and trust.'

Know? You've only known them five minutes, I thought. 'Bloody hell, it's not like you even need the money.'

'I'm not doing it for the money. I like meeting people and I've met a lot of interesting characters since I started—'

'Dealing? Surely there are safer ways to make friends,' I said. Just then the sound of gasping from one of his other friends emanated from the bedroom. 'Or maybe not.'

'Oh, give it a rest, son. I enjoy what I'm doing, who I'm meeting. Life is fun now, not like it used to be with your…'

He stopped himself before he mentioned Mum, knowing that was a step too far in front of me, especially now, but he might as well have said it, as I saw red anyway.

'You're massively breaking the law, you know. You always disagreed with this, so how can you completely go against that belief now? You're feeding addicts' drug habits. It's morally deplorable, Dad,' I said with all the hypocrisy of a casual recreational drug user who'd be stuffed without someone like Dad to get his drugs from.

'If it wasn't me doing it, it would be someone else. So you see it might as well be me. And don't you think the police know this is going on? They probably like the fact that it's someone like me.'

'Like the fact? How do you work that one out?'

'At least I will not rip these people off.'

This was the one thing he said that I could agree with. He was an honest businessman – even Brian knew that – it was just so hard to get my head around the fact that the business was not coins any longer, but drugs.

'And I only sell top quality stuff. The purer it is, the less dangerous, because it's not cut with all sorts of rubbish.'

Who is this guy? He sounded like the Godfather, not *my* father.

'I'll never sell to someone who's addicted either. I actually turned a girl away the other day because she really does need help, she's taking far too much.'

I shook my head and opened my mouth to say I was leaving.

'Do you want to try some?' He gestured to the bag of whiteish powder.

I blinked incredulously.

'God knows we could both use a little escape after that awful news. Your mum.'

For a second my anger ebbed away as I saw he was affected by Mum's diagnosis after all. But the tide soon turned again and I stropped, 'Christ, Dad, I've tried coke before.'

'Oh, it's not coke,' he said coolly, as if he was talking about brands of tea bags. 'It's crystal meth.'

He held up one of the glass pipes for my inspection and the words that dude in the bar in San Diego had whispered to my dad about menthol crystals for his cold became clear – crystal clear. But the weirdest thing about all this – my gay dad the drug dealer, holding up a crack pipe to me whilst his new gay mates banged each other's brains out in the S&M version of Alton Towers down the hall – the weirdest thing right then to me was the sound of my own voice going, 'All right then.'

CHAPTER 16.

LEARNING TO ~~DRIVE~~ FLY

Weed: OK. Everyone smokes a cigarette at some point in their life, so smoking a joint was never such a leap. Pills: hmm, all right. Everyone pops a pill for something at some point, be it paracetamol or Valium or some other pharmaceutical poison with its interminable list of side effects. What's the difference if there's a little MDMA in that pill? Cocaine: snorting something up your nose seemed like taking it to the next level – there was no routine comparison in daily life for it that I could think of, but so many people did it in the circles I moved in, in the City, in media, advertising and marketing, that it couldn't be wrong or dangerous, could it? But I'd never envisioned smoking something from a crack pipe. I didn't know anyone who had. That, for me, was one step too far, it felt like a destructive move, something you would try if you got in with that mythical *wrong crowd* your parents always warned you about, something you would do only if you'd lost all self-respect. But when it's your own dad offering you a puff, the context completely changes. When he invited me to have a try, it was like he'd asked if I wanted a cup of PG Tips – it felt like there was no danger. It couldn't have been a safer environment: I was in my dad's home, it was stuff my old man was smoking and had bought himself, and, come on, if he's doing it then why can't I? When a parent is doing something it totally takes the edge off it, right? When the aunts and uncles all get up to dance at the wedding, all us kids sit down. When your granny hums 'Wonderwall' whilst doing some knitting you know it's time to ditch Britpop. When your mum wears Ray Bans in the summer, you have to find another brand of sunglasses. But Dad had been setting a pace for the last few years that had no precedent among the fathers of anyone I knew, so I had no one to sound off to, to compare notes with, to empathise with me. To my mates like Jake and Will, Dad was both a legend and a laughing stock. He had killed the buzz of illegal things we could do as a rite of passage as well as made some of them possible. And here he was doing it again. Offering me an experience I had never tried before. There's also no denying that that moment before you do something new for the first time – whether it's jumping out of a plane, taking your first drink, driving a car on your own after passing your test or taking a new drug – the novelty itself enhances the adrenaline rush. So I admit, beneath all my frustration with Dad – perhaps *because* of all my frustration with Dad – I was both curious and excited to try the meth. It might even take the edge off this moment, I thought. With my mum terminally ill and my dad now a drug dealer, you won't be surprised to know I was feeling a little vulnerable. I felt like things were out of control, and, let's face it, that's when drugs can seem awfully medicinal.

Mum. When he had mentioned her earlier, Dad's carefree demeanour had temporarily but significantly shrivelled and it suddenly occurred to me that this whole drug dealer thing might simply be his way of kicking back against life. He'd played by the book and been so law-abiding throughout the years and what did he get in return? The mental torture of suppressing his sexuality for most of his life and the only woman he ever did love dying of cancer. Perhaps he had a point. Why the hell should he play by the rules all the time if life just spat it back in his face? And who was I to judge him for this? In fact, come to think of it, why the hell should *I* play by the rules all the time if life just spits it back in my face too?

'Let's actually find out what all the fuss is about then,' I thought. I'd heard about it on the news, seen the pictures of good-looking young people side by side with pictures of themselves after long-term meth use: the lesions on skeletal faces, the stumps for teeth inside withered lips. But like all things on the news we only ever heard the horrific side of it, never the positive. Would I get hopelessly addicted to what they declared was one of the most addictive drugs in the world? Yes, of course, there must be a risk, but I felt it was small. After all, I'd managed to prevent myself becoming dependent on all the other drugs I'd used recreationally, and I was confident I had the self-discipline and self-respect to resist this particular drug's charms. So I took hold of the proffered pipe and found myself following Dad's instructions.

'Will it fuck me up?' I said, a nervous tremor in my voice.

Dad smiled mischievously. 'No! After a few seconds you'll just feel very alert, awake, really chatty. It feels great.'

I worried for a slow-motion moment if, once entered, this was a wormhole I could never get out of again. I looked at the dustbin bags on the window which signalled that Dad knew what he was doing was wrong, but then I looked at Dad, his smile, his energy. How can *that* be wrong? The misery out there beyond the bin liners is what's wrong, I told myself, and it's all just jealous because my clever dad has found the antidote. So, mentally sticking two fingers up at the world, I said, 'Go on then.'

Dad hopped around in his seat gleefully and tapped some of the powder into the pipe.

'Can't believe I'm doing this,' I muttered, supressing a schoolboy smile.

'It's fine, honestly. Just take a small amount though because it's quite powerful.'

I sat there cradling the pipe, feeling just like I did when I held Sasithorn Sonjohnkoksoong's boobs in my hands for the first time. 'OK, now what?'

'OK,' Dad said with all the soothing authority he had used when I had first sat behind the wheel of his Cortina in an empty car park in Edgware, except this time he wasn't saying, 'I'm going to let the handbrake off again and this time you're going to press *very* gently on the accelerator and lift your foot *very* gradually off the clutch,' before we went kangarooing towards a wall. No, this time he cooed, 'So I'm going to melt the crystals with the lighter, and when I do that just breathe in the fumes.'

He flicked on his Zippo with startling skill and the flame quickly blackened the bottom of the pipe. I watched the crystals inside melt into a colourless liquid, smoke filling up the glass bowl. And finally I inhaled it.

I waited.

It didn't take long. The best way I could describe the feeling was a sudden rush; not overwhelming, but a strong, intense buzz. My senses felt heightened, I was incredibly alert, I felt really good, wanted to chat, had this urge to socialise with whoever was there, happy to discuss any topic that was up for discussion, or learn anything that was there to be learnt – but given that the only other people around were the gimps in the other room spit-roasting some twink, I decided that the best topics up for discussion and greatest things to be learnt were right now here in this little office.

The high took all my anxieties about what Dad was doing, rolled them up into a big squishy ball in my chest and fired them through every single one of my neurons out into space. I felt wonderfully anaesthetised to the rest of the world and compelled to connect with my father on a level I had only done with mates before, the danger I had identified a few minutes before now only serving to enhance each rush.

If I could compare it to anything, doing meth was similar to my experience of a good pill, but somehow more controllable, which was definitely a plus. The essence of the euphoria did have similarities to E. One of the differences with meth was the almost instant gratification, and then, once it wore off, the same immediate hit could be obtained again simply by another toke on the pipe. But there was no doubt I'd never experienced anything quite like it, and it was a close call between that and E as being the most powerful and seductive of the drugs I'd tried.

Dad's voice came out of the haze: 'Well, how do you feel?'

'Fucking good,' I said, caressing my own stomach. 'Wow, that's strong.' I luxuriated in the feeling for a moment before finding the energy to say, 'No wonder people get addicted to this shit.'

Dad laughed uproariously. 'It's incredible, isn't it?' Then in more sober tones he quickly added, 'I'm not proud that I'm giving this to you, by the way.'

'Don't worry about it, Dad. I'm old enough to be making these decisions for myself now,' I said as if I was talking about what subjects I would take for GCSE or how often to attend the synagogue. 'I'm obviously going to be curious, with all this going on here. But I wouldn't be doing it if I didn't want to.'

'Well, OK, but just be careful.'

Be careful. Oh, the irony of your dad's expressions of parental responsibility as he holds a flame to your crack pipe!

'Shut up, Dad!' I tutted, eager to try and claw back a bit of control over one of the days in my life that had never felt so out of my hands. 'I'm not a baby. I have done stuff like this before,' I lied.

'Well, I'm not exactly being the best dad in the world by encouraging this, am I?'

'It's my choice,' I insisted, not for the last time that evening. But even as I repeated the words I wondered if all of this was, in fact, out of my hands.

That night I was unable to sleep. The insomnia, it turned out, was one of the downsides of the drug. Feeling a bit fucked up back in my flat on my own was no fun. I'd left Dad's place late that night and now, early the following morning, I was home alone with no one to share the comedown. There was the small matter of the news of my dad being a drug dealer that was probably adding to the insomnia, but right then it was easier to focus on the effects of the drug and the experience of doing it with Dad – and they were both undoubtedly out of this world, in so many ways.

CHAPTER 17

BEETHOVEN AND THE BRUTALISTS

Despite the absolute downer after my first night on meth, I was, like most other humans, stunningly amnesiac when it comes to the negative effects of drugs and alcohol. How many times back in the day had I woken up under the kitchen table with a tongue the same texture as our neglected carpets and the sensation of someone with very well-made Doc Martens kicking at my eyeballs from the inside? How many times had I crawled out from said table to find Jake or Will or both of them curled up uncomfortably on the sofa beside a soup of vomit and spliff butts in the massive ashtray, stolen from the local pub, like most of our considerable collection of glasses? And yet a few days later (if not a few hours) we'd be back on the booze, or whatever narcotics we'd been abusing, as if it was our first time, as if we had no idea that we would once again, and utterly self-inflicted, feel like shit the following morning. When it came to getting blasted we had all the memory capacity of goldfish – goldfish in an aquarium filled with lager where those little pretty-coloured stones on the bottom were ecstasy pills and that weed growing up from between them was, erm, weed. And now we – correction, *I* – had another tool of self-harm to add to the tank: gurgling up from that little pump in the corner that's supposed to filter the water were bubbles bursting with gases produced from burning crystals of methamphetamine.

So I found myself heading back to Dad's the following week in a manner not unlike Dory from *Finding Nemo*, which I'd sat through in the cinema just days before to please Vicki, although the comparison was totally lost on my twenty-five-year-old self. Not surprisingly, Dad was busy 'working'. But since the cat was out of the bag now as far his *supplying* went, I invited myself into the office this time and sat there in a bizarre perversion of my childhood days at the shop in Regent Street as Dad chatted and dealt crystal meth to Roger, a film set designer. Roger was a man of diminutive stature, wore round glasses and had a warm, genial manner – a bit like if Doc from the Seven Dwarves was a meth head. He chatted with me and Dad about his job and, perhaps inevitably for his line of work, dropped names of A-list celebs he'd befriended. I liked Roger though, mainly because it never felt like he was mentioning these names to show off – it was simply the truth, so why shouldn't he say it? Roger dressed well, was successful in his field and didn't look one inch the image of a meth user the media liked to paint.

I watched, fascinated, as Dad deftly kept the conversation going whilst measuring out a couple of grams of powder onto his weighing scales, bagging it up and taking the money Roger handed over with the same innocent air he used to weigh coins and trade over the desk in Regent Street. I sat next to Dad feeling this weird buzz as the conversation flowed with a surface ease, the deal to be done always shimmering in the depths like pirate treasure. I flattered myself that I was one of Dr No's henchmen, my now bald father only short of a scar and a white pussy to pass for the arch villain, although in actual fact I was probably more akin to a mere Bond girl, set dressing, if Bond girls were scrawny, spotty Jews with penises.

The living room felt more like a GP's waiting room these days, scattered with various people as it was, waiting their turn to get their prescription. Keith was next in line and, when Roger left, I happily called him in, at my father's request, like some doe-eyed receptionist. Keith, it turned out, ran a ship-salvaging business. He would scour old ships, recover furniture, artefacts and valuables, and then trade them on the market. I was fascinated. It was straight out of *Titanic*, steeped in history and ghosts of the past. Keith had hands as tough as old mooring ropes, but he had done well for himself and was able to leave most of the scouring to his staff these days – another antithesis of the drug-using clichés I'd expected to find stumbling through Dad's flat. Investment bankers, artists and members of the medical profession filed through, most very successful, clean and well kempt, not the gaunt, skeletal, dirty crack whores I'd expected. Even Frank, the manager of the apartment block, popped in and not, as you might expect, to tell Dad to refrain from making his block into a den of iniquity, but to score his own few grams of the good stuff.

'I've got someone very special who I'd like you meet on Sunday, Richard,' Frank grinned as he received his little bag of powder.

'Oh yes?' Dad said. 'Who?'

Frank looked at me and then over his shoulder at the waiting room. 'Maximum discretion required, so I'll keep schtum for now, and mum's the word when you meet him too, Richard, OK?'

'OK,' Dad said, looking both excited and somewhat miffed that he was not trusted with the identity of Frank's presumably high-profile friend yet. 'Mum's the word.'

Mum's the word. Mum, the word, shook my soul like a frantic lover trying to revive a suicidal partner; trying to tell me… something; trying to tell me I had somewhere far more important to be, with someone who needed me more than these libertines, but right then I was too caught up, too pleasantly numb to reality to move.

Frank left and I fidgeted, anticipating hearing from Dad who this mystery person was after their meeting on Sunday, so no doubt I would be back as soon as possible to find out. Meanwhile Dad, being Dad, closed up shop, always at the same hour each evening, not too late, and I looked forward to this time the most when we just got to hang out and chat one-to-one, father and son – with a few puffs on the meth pipe, of course.

As soon as he was high, Dad couldn't wait to show me his latest high-tech discovery.

'Have you seen this, son?' he beamed as he typed the URL into his laptop. 'It's called YouTube.'

I laughed warmly but patronisingly to remind him I was in digital marketing so of course I knew about YouTube, which had been launched in the previous year and was already revolutionising the way the world consumed visual media.

'You can find anything you want on here,' Dad said. 'It's amazing. I don't know how it all gets on there, but it's there. Look! All I have to do is type something here and…' He punched return and proceeded to show me clips of his favourite opera singers and live performances of his most prized classical pieces by the world's greatest orchestras. Since I was high too by now I was ravenous for extra stimulation, gagging to absorb anything he cared to show me. And there was lots he wanted to show. One clip had barely begun before he clicked onto another, and another, his finger trying to keep up as his speeding brain flitted from one thought to the next.

I smiled a lunatic smile as this ADHD tour through the best of Baroque sent flashes of a past life through me. I felt, on and off for stretched split seconds, that I was floating through one of Keith's salvaged ghost ships, except instead of cabins full of maritime artefacts I was passing through our old semi in suburban London with the smells of Mum cooking up a matzoh ball soup tickling my nostrils while Dad sipped on Earl Grey and put another Handel cassette in the tape player. And I smiled a lunatic smile because I knew that this hint of the old life was brought to me today courtesy of a class A narcotic called crystal meth.

These thoughts of the past sent random pangs of melancholy and even vague panic shooting through me, competing with the rushes of exhilaration – not a healthy combination – but I tried to suppress the negative feelings for now, desperate to stay in the moment and ride the crest of this narcotic awakening.

And it wasn't long before Dad segued into clips of Lisa Lashes and Tony De Vit dropping some bangers at hard house nights around the world, the contrast to the previous genre of music sending me into hysterics.

My also-speeding brain couldn't resist any longer. 'Check this out, Dad,' I said, cutting in and pulling up a live track of The Darkness from the US tour we had seen a part of. 'Remember this?'

'Oh yeah,' he said, playing air guitar in a way which, on any other day in the past, would have induced embarrassment in me of mortifying proportions, but now just had me rushing with a sense of bonding.

Deep in the troughs between euphoric tokes on the meth pipe I would start to worry. Worry about Dad getting caught for dealing drugs, worry about Dad getting hooked on drugs and killing himself, worry about myself getting arrested for just being here when Dad was dealing – does that make me an accessory after the fact? But then I'd take another draw on that tantalising smoke curling up from the little bubbling cauldron between my fingers and I'd think, 'If this is the only way I can feel close to Dad these days, then I'm not about to walk away from that. And if he is intent on pursuing this lifestyle, surely it's better I stick around to make sure he's all right, rather than abandoning him to God knows what and God knows who.'

We enjoyed many nights like that at his flat. We didn't go out together that much, mainly due to his inability to make arrangements, stick to them, remember them, and then, even if he did remember them, turn up at all close to the pre-agreed time. This tardiness was a trait of his throughout his whole life, at least as far back as I can remember, and one of the things that tended to drive Mum up the wall. She was the opposite, always turning up five or ten minutes early; she couldn't stand being even a minute late. So it was no surprise this was a source of tension throughout the marriage. And when you mix drugs, a healthy dose of depression and a generally chaotic lifestyle, the situation was exacerbated ten-fold.

But there were a few exceptions. The one that stands out is our trip to the Barbican to watch Beethoven's Seventh Symphony, the merits of which both Dad and I agreed upon. I managed to mitigate his usual lateness by arranging to come to his flat first and he would then drive there, so I was able to hustle him along and have an element of control over the situation.

We parked the car relatively quickly and easily for the City and, just like all those times in Tesco, he was bouncing with a disproportionate sense of triumph.

'How incredible to get a space there, eh, son? Would never have thought that could happen! At this time of day and on a Friday night too! They must have added more parking spaces. Or no one's out tonight for some reason. But why would everyone be at home on a night like this? All that talk of a recession probably. People staying at home and saving their money.'

'OK, Dad, it doesn't matter why,' I said, virtually dragging him from the car.

What mattered to me, what shocked me, in fact, was that we were actually on time for the start of the performance – we even had a little time to spare. Time for me, as we took our seats, to scan the people around us and marvel at the demographic of the audience: uniformly white, of course, mostly over fifty, speaking with a loud irreverence for the space, cultivated from years and years of exposure to similar events, in voices filed sharp by posh accents. I felt a thrill at being one of them and a slight resentment at feeling like an imposter, especially since I was now the son of a drug dealer. And yet I was glad to be infiltrating the ranks of these ruling classes, strangely satisfied to be intruding on and contaminating their entitled little bubble.

Their irreverence for the space was countered by an unquestioning and rather dumb veneration for the music which, like blind religious faith, irked my atheist self, although in the case of Beethoven's Seventh I was in equal awe and as the room throbbed with the opening phrases I couldn't help but compare the big, bold stabs from the strings punctuating the legato woodwind lines to the rushes and floaty highs of a ride on meth. But the spine-tingling that was going on here was all achieved without the aid of narcotics and so it was, without doubt, a million times more special.

As the lights dimmed before the conductor first raised his baton, the audience had delivered that symphony of plague-like coughing that is *de rigueur* before settling down to any performance in a theatre space, except Dad had continued coughing throughout. The second, quieter, movement began with its familiar theme, which half the audience waved a hand or pom-pommed their lips to in order to try and convince the rest of us that they were connoisseurs of the entire symphony, and Dad's lung hacking became a lot more noticeable. Various heavily made-up or thickly eye-browed faces were turned in our direction, expressions like melted riding boots. I smiled apologetically at them and nudged Dad, who tried desperately to keep the hawking under control, but like a giggle in a strict teacher's classroom, the more he tried to keep it quiet the more it wanted to announce itself to the entire room and get him into trouble.

The interval couldn't come soon enough. I ushered Dad out of the auditorium and we went out to the enormous paved patio out back where most of the punters went during the break. There were giant square ponds there boasting synchronised fountains all surrounded on high by the offices and residences of the Barbican, a beacon of Brutalist architecture, as attractive as a multi-storey car park. I believe this garden space was designed to continue the perception that you were experiencing a level of high culture, such as that you would have just absorbed in the retro-futuristic interior, somehow facilitating intellectual conversation on the key highlights (or lowlights) of what had just been witnessed. But Dad and I found it was a good place to find a concrete perch in a quiet corner in which to have a few puffs on the meth pipe. I felt like a school kid behind the bike shed trying to get in a few sneaky tokes of a cigarette before we got caught. We were completely separated from the rest of the gin-and-tonic toting crowd, not just by an unpopulated expanse of cement paving, but, it seemed, by the very nature of what we deemed acceptable now. We were in a different universe, and I had to say I liked the feeling of being other. Although we probably looked to them like a couple of scaggy heroin-addicted losers, I nurtured a feeling of superiority to this stiff, sheltered herd.

I drew on the pipe and the fumes that permeated my lungs emboldened me to ask Dad about that person Frank, the manager of his apartment block, was supposed to have introduced him to last Sunday; the one he was supposed to remain tight-lipped about.

'So tell me, Dad, who was this mystery person you were hanging out with on Sunday?'

'Oh, just some… musician. Was that the call for the second half to start?'

Nice try, Dad, but I wasn't about to be put off the scent. 'No, we've got ages yet. Can't you tell me who it is?'

'Another toke?'

'Thanks.' I took the pipe and, as Dad hoped, that silenced me for a while, but only for a few seconds.

'Dad, you can tell me, you know. I'm not going to blurt it out to anyone at all. This is all in the strictest confidence.'

I watched Dad's face. Watched him waver. I knew I nearly had him. My curiosity was swelling to dangerous proportions. Curiosity. So many points in this story, it seems, have turned on curiosity. Dad and Mum's sexuality perhaps, the discoveries I made in Dad's office and his second bedroom for sure, Dad trying drugs, me trying drugs. And we all know what curiosity did, don't we?

'I think we better go back in. Don't want to miss the rest, eh?'

'Dad.' It was time to play my trump card. 'If you can't tell your only son, who can you tell?'

Dad took one last toke on the pipe, inhaled deeply looking up at the grey apartment blocks all around us, and I was suddenly gripped by a sense of observing a convict looking over prison walls – but that could have just been the oppressive nature of the concrete jungle around us.

'You really have to promise me that you won't tell anyone. I mean it, James. I'll be really upset if I hear it's got out.'

Bingo!

'Of course, absolutely promise, you've got my word. Who was it?'

Dad opened his mouth to speak, but instead of the name I'd been waiting for he coughed violently and an alien green blob of expectorate shot out onto the ground.

'Nice.'

'Sorry, son.'

'Are you OK?' I said, putting a hand on Dad's arm and being quite shocked at the scarcity of meat I found on his bones. I had seen him slimming down since he'd started his new life, but this was going too far. 'Are you OK?' I said again, hoping he knew somehow I was referring to his weight this time.

'I'm fine. Let's go in!' he said, jumping up energetically to show me just how fine he was.

'Hang on! You're not getting away with it that easily.'

'What?' he said coyly.

'Dish the dirt! Who did you meet?'

'Oh.' He leant over and whispered the name.

'Really?' I squealed. Dad had just delivered a bona fide, twenty-four carat, A-list, pop music icon name-drop into my ear.

Dad was surprised by my reaction. 'You know who that is?'

'Of course I bloody well know who that is. Who doesn't know who that is?'

'Well, I didn't really. Not at first. Frank just invited me round to the bloke's house in Hampstead.'

'You've been to…' I had to restrain myself from shouting this out, a cry which would have echoed around the massive concrete courtyard for longer than this singer's favourite studio effect. '… *His* house?'

'Yes.'

Now, I know you'll be dying, as I was, to find out exactly who this celebrity was, but come on, you heard me, I swore I wouldn't tell a soul – wink emoji.

'And what did you do at his house?' I said, knowing this particular singer was out and proud just like my dad, but not believing for a second they could have actually got up to anything. Well, not together, directly, anyway. That would have been just too weird for words.

'Well, we smoked a little…' He waved the pipe at me and pocketed it.

'Meth? You did meth with…?'

Dad nodded, coy again.

'Just you and him?'

'No, there was Frank and a few other blokes I'd never met before. It was funny really because as we chatted everyone realised I'd never really heard of him – or his music, anyway. "Is it techno or hard house?" I asked. And the guy shook his head. "Well, I wouldn't have heard of it then," I said and everyone fell about. But I never really listened to pop music, did I. So he started putting his records on. "Have you heard this one before, Richard?" he went. "No," I said. "OK, what about this one?"

"No, never, sorry." "Oh, come on, Richard," he goes, becoming increasingly flustered. "You must know this one. How about this one? It was *huge*.'"

'Oh my God.' I laughed, mouth agape. 'You totally dissed one of the most successful singers in UK pop history.'

'Well, I didn't mean to,' Dad said with a wonderfully genuine naivety.

I think the call for the second half to begin really did ring out at that point, but I had to know more about Dad's evening with this star. Dad told me the singer was lamenting the rough treatment he always got from the press, and that Dad was consoling him over it. I could imagine Dad doing just that. He was always a good listener, and was good at saying the right thing. He'd spent most of his adult life in therapy, and as a result had a theory for almost any type of behaviour, rightly or wrongly, as he was no trained therapist himself, of course. But it seemed to work on people, and it sounded good, plausible. Dad had told his new A-list friend something along the lines that the harsh treatment he was getting was a reflection of people's envy, jealousy of his talent and success, and he should completely ignore it. He had a point, and I think it went down well. They obviously got on famously (excuse the pun) because the singer had invited Dad back to hang out at his Hampstead mansion again. He even had a text to prove it.

Throughout my life, I've seen people gravitate towards Dad: they love his company. He's sociable, an extrovert but also a very empathetic character (which is surprising for someone whose habits lie on the border of autism), and it's always been one of the elements of his personality I most strongly admired. So I felt proud of this latest example of it, especially since it was demonstrated for and with someone who could presumably choose from a multitude of people to spend his time with.

'You know, the funny thing is,' Dad said as we wandered back inside for another dose of Beethoven, but hopefully not another bout of coughing, 'I think he's quite lonely, a little bit lost. I felt quite sorry for him. It's surprising really, with all that money, that playboy lifestyle, that success.'

That oppressive low came over me again as Dad spoke, because he could have been speaking about himself. But just then the meth took another joyride through the backstreets of my body and I was buzzing on the news that my dad was getting high with—

No, I can't say. I'd be as bad as a tabloid paper if I did. Full of gossip and scandal, those filthy rags. Look, it's gossip and *careless whispers* that get people into trouble, so though I'd been *waiting for that day* when Dad would tell me, I decided it would be best to leave that titbit *outside* where my *father (figure)* told me to leave it, in what now seemed a somewhat *different corner* of the Barbican patio. Double wink emoji.

CHAPTER 18

PRESTIGE CARS AND LAVENDER FARTS

It was easier to get high with Dad than get low with Mum, but I visited her, of course, perhaps more regularly than ever. At least at first.

Just two weeks after the diagnosis she was having major surgery. Ruth and Mum had decided to go private since cancer cells didn't really care for NHS waiting lists; when it came to killing people they tended to push in at the front of the queue, so why the hell shouldn't Mum do that too?

The surgery was at the Portland Hospital. It would be a total abdominal hysterectomy. Dad, Ruth and I all went along, and as Mum went off to theatre I tried to make the final look we exchanged as contented and peaceful as I could for both of us, just in case it was the last we ever had – I was terrified that there would be some major complication and it would be the procedure and not the cancer that would end up killing her prematurely. The three of us sat in the waiting area, biting nails, fidgeting and reading magazines that we'd never touch in a million years usually, and I kept replaying the way Mum smiled at me as they wheeled her away – it was the unsteady smile of a mum reassuring her son, when frankly she had far bigger things to worry about.

Then, all too soon, the surgeon came and beckoned Ruth over. Beckoned Ruth, not Dad, not even me. It was a moment that stuck and reminded me how this family had changed. Not that I resented Ruth being told first. Actually, I was relieved, as it gave me the chance to bury my head in the sand a little longer. But she soon came and relayed the news: 'Operation went as well as could have been expected... a major operation... recovering in intensive care... we can visit her shortly.'

Shortly? What, as in now, *today*? I was glad the operation had gone smoothly, but I wasn't sure I was ready to see my mum so soon after such a trauma to her body. Only two of us should go and see her, the doctor said, in order to limit numbers in the ward. This could have been my perfect get out, and yet it was Dad who volunteered to stay behind.

For once, my geekish self was not amused with the view afforded me by the sci-fi tinted spectacles through which I tended to see the world. There were wires coming out of her like alien tendrils and tubes going into her with the unfeeling intrusiveness of the artificial. It stopped me in my tracks. It punched me in the stomach. It shouted at me to grow up, but I didn't want to hear that because it meant that this little soldier's mummy was slipping away. As skilful and as well-intentioned as the surgeon was, his knife had removed the most significant part of her that made my mum my mum – the womb that had grown and incubated me.

After the wires had been removed and Mum was recovered, from the surgery at least, the doctors decided that it was time to pump her with drugs and toxins to a level that even Dad would struggle to consume. Ironic really, since the most damaging cocktail she'd probably ever taken in her life so far was wine and paracetamol. This was where my visits to her, in hospital anyway, stopped being so regular. In fact, they stopped altogether. But this was Mum's choice. She said she didn't want me to see her going through the chemotherapy. 'No son should ever see his mother go through that,' she said. She went to the hospital once a week for this voluntary poisoning. I watched her go from a relatively well-looking cancer sufferer to a ravaged one. And it was the chemo that did it. A lot of people think that that heroin chic cancer look is only achieved by the liberal application of cancer cells themselves, but the reality is that a lot of the time, it is the chemo that you really need for that maximum *Trainspotting* effect. And my mum nailed it. Then they pumped her full of steroids to combat the sickness, and so she bloated. Along with the loss of her long, black hair, she was left looking just like the stereotype of a lesbian I had once feared Ruth would be before she'd opened the door to Beth and me just a few years ago. Of course, now I knew time was precious,

I was always taking photos or videos of Mum, and though she would never stop me from capturing these memories, I could tell she was a little embarrassed of the way she looked. I found Mum sitting at her mirror one day, slapping on the blusher to try and cover up her now tired, pale skin.

'I look like Coco the bloody Clown,' she sighed.

And my heart cracked.

Twelve weeks later, in the middle of the last course of chemo, she came out in a worrying rash. The nurses immediately stopped the machines, and that was that. Mum's body had taken as much punishment as it was able to; this was biology's way of saying, 'STOP!' We hoped it had been worth it.

A couple of months later and she actually seemed more or less back to full fitness – apart from the tingling in her fingers and toes, the nerve damage which left her a little less dexterous and left idiots in the queue behind her at the ATM or the post office tutting with impatience as she struggled to handle banknotes or documents. It was October 2007. My thirtieth birthday was that month and Mum and Ruth had decided to treat me and Vicki to a no-expenses-spared trip to Provence, in the South of France. I wasn't sure we should be celebrating my birthday with all that had happened, but Mum had always loved lavender fields, the visual beauty and the fragrance of the flower, and the lavender fields of Provence were a definite on her bucket list. So it was as much about celebrating Mum feeling better (even if it was only temporary) as celebrating my birthday. And of course, it's only as you grow older that you realise your birthday is probably more significant to your parents than to you.

Mum seemed so much better, in fact, that I would often allow myself to dream that she was actually about to experience a miraculous remission, although deep down I knew how unlikely, if not impossible, that was. I knew this could well be one of, if not *the*, last proper holiday I would spend with her. That terrible feeling of finality, last chances, last moments was almost too unbearable to face. How precious time was, but how frustrating that it only felt precious during times like these! The pressure to make the most of every moment was emotionally draining. It all had to be perfect and if it wasn't there was no second chance to make it right. Everything felt symbolic, like moments in a cheesy Channel 5 movie, but at the same time my life had never felt so vital or real as it did now.

It seemed almost wrong to get excited about the holiday, but Vicki and I both were – especially when we found out we were booked to stay at the Four Seasons, one of the most upmarket hotel chains in the world, in one of the most beautiful parts of Europe. Vicki was still a student and I hadn't long left the flat with Jake and Will, where we had done a really great impression of being students. Neither of us had the kind of disposable income necessary to buy a holiday in the Four Seasons' laundry room, let alone the entire villa we found ourselves in a few weeks later, with Mum and Ruth next door. The bowl of exotic fruit on our lounge table (yes, our lounge, as opposed to our room) looked as if it had been specially sourced by Oompa Loompas from deepest Loompaland and the comprehensive set of bathroom toiletries, which vastly outnumbered everything we had on our own shelves at home, included lotions for doing things to parts of the body I didn't even know existed.

So while Vicki got on with decaffeinating her glabellas, or whatever it was she was doing to wherever it was she was doing it, I got on with calling room service with all the gusto that Jake and I used to call sex chat lines when we were young. OK, younger. OK, not that long ago. Anyway, I'd have room service deliver breakfast to us on our private, sun-kissed balcony every day before we met up with Mum and Ruth for an exhausting morning ordering drinks and reading our respective airport paperbacks by the pool.

During those mornings I'd stare stealthily through my shades as I sucked on a Mojito, or peek over the top of my book as I pretended to read, at Mum and Ruth on their sun loungers pulled close together chatting and joking like they'd just met, and I'd find myself stretching out like a well-fed cat as I chalked up one of those perfect moments.

I'd then challenge Vicki to a game of tennis, get all competitive à la McEnroe and spend lunch stropping into my *soupe au pistou* after yet another spanking. In the afternoon it was more sunbathing, or sometimes we managed to prise our foie gras off the loungers and actually see some of the country beyond the walls of this hotel, followed by a dinner at a Michelin-starred restaurant.

I wondered, given the level of enjoyment, ease and pleasure we were experiencing every day, if I'd end up with some form of depression once the holiday was over and I was back to the rat race. It was hard to remember sometimes that this might well be the last holiday I would ever take with my mum. But that was probably a good thing, because that way there was no drama, no tears to spoil all this fun. Every moment with her was now precious; I wanted all of them to be golden ones. Clearly so did Mum. She was more than happy. No longer that sad clown sighing into the mirror, she was the class clown now, awesomely naughty, wonderfully juvenile. She was herself again and that was a triumph.

'Come on, Vicki, hurry hurry!' she shouted from the backseat of our prestige hire car as I fired up the powerful engine, Ruth making herself comfortable up front next to me.

Vicki had been delayed by yet another change of outfit – after all, it was difficult to decide what would look best against a backdrop of purple, for we were off to the lavender farm. Mum had been munching excitedly on a packet of biscuits as we waited and had made a right mess of the upholstery with her crumbs. I told her off, but instead of sweeping them out of the car she waited for Vicki to get in and then as we drove off she said, 'Oh Vicki, look at all the mess you've brought in with you.'

Vicki was a little confused, but mostly embarrassed at being scolded by Mum. She also started checking her very carefully selected skirt to make sure she hadn't sat in something before getting in the car.

'Oh, what a mucky pup you are.' Mum persisted in the charade and Vicki went redder and redder until we all started giggling and put her out of her misery.

'Only teasing,' Mum said, giving Vicki a loving squeeze and finishing off with a gleeful fart, which we all protested loudly about, but, having wound all the windows down to expel the stench, secretly delighted in, because we could see Mum was so deliriously happy.

When we got to the farm, we did the tour, visited the shop where you could buy all things lavender, so many things lavender; things that I didn't even know it was possible to make from lavender, things that you could only possibly be tempted to buy if you were perhaps a bee who'd put his job before anything else in his life to such an extent that he was now attending Lavender Anonymous meetings at the local hive every week. After emerging from the shop smelling like a nan's bathroom we had a walk around the fields themselves. Having nearly overdosed on lavender I didn't hang around too long, but as I walked back to the car park I looked over my shoulder at Mum.

She was standing in the field alone, gazing over this vast purple crop, drinking it in, as if attempting to inhale every molecule of the scent, absorb every nanosecond of that moment, searing that image she was so enjoying onto her brain in such a vital way that I would struggle to comprehend, that perhaps anyone without a terminal illness would struggle to comprehend, not knowing that this, for sure, would be the last time they would ever perceive such a thing.

CHAPTER 19

PORTRAIT OF THE DEALER AS A LOST SOUL

I had tried to call Dad a few times from France but there had been no answer. This was not unusual. In fact it was becoming increasingly usual, but it didn't stop me worrying about him. Worrying, since his health had clearly been deteriorating recently, that I might one day turn up to find him lying dead in a pool of his own drug-induced vomit – which would increase record sales and enhance your own mythical status no end if you were rock star Jim Morrison or guitar legend Jimi Hendrix – but it would do nothing for ex-coin dealer, ex-heterosexual Richard Lubbock of Limehouse. I also worried about Dad's safety having an 'open house' for drug users as he did. I mean, many of the people I had seen coming and going from the flat had seemed nice enough, but you never know. Drug users can become drug addicts, and drug addicts can become desperate people and desperate people can do desperate things. And then there was the fact that the more and more customers he got the more the word would spread, perhaps as far as the fuzz, and he might get arrested. A terrible thought cut through my anxiety then: perhaps it wouldn't be so bad if he got arrested. It would stop him using, so he'd be free of the threat of a messy drug-induced death, and he'd be free of dealing and all the associated risks from potentially unhinged customers.

Every time I walked towards that block of flats, all that chattering anxiety walked with me. Then I'd ring the buzzer. And wait. And wait, while chattering anxiety went on and on at me in my ear like some busybody neighbour. And every time Dad's voice would come through the intercom, pleasurably distorted, I'd leave chattering anxiety shivering on the pavement while I skipped with relief into the lift and up to the seventeenth floor.

The flat seemed to get busier every time I visited. People milling about like some high-end halfway house; some waiting for their turn to buy drugs from Dad in the office, some waiting for a go in the sex room, others just sitting around chatting, socialising, as if down the pub, a place where lonely souls could come together and find comfort. There was even a French artist who was taking over the lounge with his collection of 'in progress' paintings. Karol had appropriately wild, long, black hair and strutted around the flat topless, showing off his hugely protruding nipples, one of which was pierced, and both of which could have served as coat hangers. Despite his intimidating level of bohemianism he was always friendly and effusive, and I liked him. When he was there he gave the flat a more respectable feel, despite his semi-nakedness; turned it into a creative hang-out that wasn't so subversive. And while he was also there for the drugs, of course, and perhaps the odd go on the swing, at least he had a passion which was life affirming. Among his paintings he was even working on a portrait of Dad. You could see Dad's trademark blue tank top, from which his skinny arms emerged, his head resting on one hand. The features of his face were not finished yet and I watched with fascination as Karol applied the paint with virtuosic abandon.

I was on first-name terms with many of the people hanging around now: the set designer Roger, and Keith the ship salvager among them.

'How are you, James?'

'Good, Keith. You?'

'I'm fine, but I was wondering about your dad.'

'Oh yeah?'

'Yeah. He seems to be doing quite a lot of meth himself these days. He needs to keep an eye on that.'

My first instinct was to be riled by a meth head – even if it was a fascinating ship-salvaging meth head – telling me my dad was doing too much meth. But then a more rational me thought, well, if a meth head thinks Dad is doing too much meth, perhaps that speaks volumes. So I found myself opening up a little to Keith.

'I know,' I sighed. 'I worry, but what can I do? I can't make him stop.'

Keith nodded sympathetically, but ploughed on, 'And he really needs to be more careful with what's going on, you know. He doesn't seem to have any discretion these days. I mean, even with the window in his room – he should properly cover that up, people can see right in.'

'I know. I try to tell him but it just falls on deaf ears.'

'And to be honest, some of the people I've seen coming and going recently, they look dodgy, troublemakers. He has to be careful who he deals with.'

'He keeps telling me they're all trustworthy, that he knows them—'

'When you get people recommending people recommending people, discretion is going to go down the swanny, James.'

'Sure. But what can I do?'

Now I felt angry because I felt bloody guilty – guilty that strangers were advising me that Dad was in a bad, potentially dangerous, situation, and I, his son, his own flesh and blood, wasn't able to do anything about it. Of course I wanted the whole thing to stop, but how?

I consulted friends, agonising over how far I should go to stop Dad's seemingly unstoppable journey to self-destruction. Will suggested giving Dad an ultimatum: I would not see him again until he ceased this madness. Sadly, I came to the conclusion that his immersion in the 'scene' and his addiction was twisting his personality and sense of judgement to such an extent that he would most likely choose the drugs over me. Jake suggested an even more extreme approach: pay someone to impersonate a police officer who would pay a visit to Dad's flat and give him a final warning – essentially, scare the living Jesus out of him. But if he'd found out that that was my doing, would he ever forgive me in his current state? It was a Chinese puzzle – even worse, a Jewish Chinese puzzle – and I had no idea how to solve it, so I resigned myself to making the most of my time with him, which I feared would be limited due to his failing health. Right up to the end I still harboured fantasies that Dad would suddenly see sense, stop what he was doing and slowly work his way back to normality. It was just a phase, he just needed to get it out of his system, I told myself, like a prissy parent watching their teenage boy stomp out of the house in eyeliner and full Goth attire.

I sat there as Karol put the finishing touches to Dad's portrait, the face now fully rendered with an expression of utter melancholy and eyes that seemed moist with welling tears: the face of a lost soul who could blink it all away in an instant to play the host with the most, everyone's new best friend.

CHAPTER 20

THE SHADOW
BETWEEN THE TREES

The agency I worked for was not very impressed when I said I was going on another holiday so soon after the one to Provence, but I didn't really give a toss: Mum had called from Vermont where she was staying with Ruth at her house there and invited me over to spend a week with them. These days, an invitation from Mum was not something I would put second to anything – I was not going to be that person who wished he'd spent more time with his loved ones while he had the chance.

As well as the week in Vermont, the plan was then to meet Vicki in New York City for a couple of days of sightseeing and partying with friends we knew there – all paid for again by Mum and Ruth, including a few nights in the plush Gansevoort Hotel in the trendy Meatpacking District of Manhattan.

I realised all this money spent on me was partly guilt-driven. As many parents would, I think Mum was trying to compensate me for a hurt she believed she had caused me by becoming ill. She must have felt there was no other way to make amends in such a helpless situation. Of course, I didn't require her to make amends of any sort, but I made bloody sure that I would make the most of the experiences she was offering me and the precious time she was buying us together, for both our sakes.

When I arrived at JFK Airport I was met by a driver, Ruth's very own driver. Just as well, as it was a six-hour drive to their place in the neighbouring state. Jackson, the driver, was a long-time employee of Ruth's and a very friendly chap. Very talkative, larger than life and far up one end of the spectrum of maleness – the other end to the one Julian Clary would be found at, for example. Consequently he regaled me with the many female conquests he had made in his life. And, as the list grew ever longer over the course of the six-hour journey, culminating with talk of an old flame recently reignited, whose beauty, apparently after all these years, Jackson was delighted to confirm, had barely diminished – or as he put it, 'I tell ya, her tits still pointed straight up to Jesus!' – I felt, despite, the sexual security Vicki had given me, that I too, by comparison with such a stud as Jackson, inhabited those far reaches of the spectrum that the mincer Mr Clary did.

Thanks to Jackson, the car journey up (and back down a week later) went very quickly indeed, but I was still relieved to get to my destination, and it was an emotional reunion, even if it had only been a couple of months since I last saw Mum in Provence.

This time we enjoyed some of the attractions Vermont had to offer – dry tobogganing (which is not as sore as it sounds), the local cinema, and I even allowed Mum to take me clothes shopping, despite my fear of coming out of the stores looking like Pee-wee Herman all over again, when I was just beginning to learn how to dress like an adult, as opposed to a child who'd raided the dressing-up box. We also took long walks through the world-class natural beauty of the reds and browns and yellows of a late Vermont autumn. We rambled through local woods that looked like oil paintings, opening out onto crystal-clear blue lakes, mirrors to the sky. At one point I realised I was having to work quite hard to keep up with Mum's pace.

'She's so fit, so strong. How can she have terminal cancer?' I thought to myself, toying with the idea that maybe she was cured, perhaps a miracle had happened after all. Or, if not cured, then surely she had increased her time significantly given her current state of health and the aggressive treatment she'd had to date.

But then one day we were playing crazy golf – not exactly what you travel to Vermont for, I know, but we knew it would give us a laugh, and we were all about finding the laughs now, more than ever. Since this course was called Lots O' Balls we were off to a good start and Mum and I sniggered like a couple of schoolkids for ages about that. However, halfway round she was teeing up to negotiate a giant concrete toadstool, and as she took position, she stumbled. There were no bumps or divots, she was just a little unsteady on her feet. She giggled, remarking how useless she was at the game in an attempt to brush it aside, but I knew as well as she did that it was a symptom of the chemo, which affects your nervous system and therefore your balance. It was a sad reminder of her illness and it was always there in the background, trying to undermine our fun.

The week passed quickly, too quickly. We said our goodbyes and, though we reassured ourselves that it would not be long until we saw each other again back home in London, my journey back to New York would have been wracked with doubt had I not had the Hugh Hefner of chauffeurs to keep me amused and distracted all the way.

As I partied with Vicki and friends among the neoned rooftops of Manhattan I would catch myself in brief moments of melancholy, marvelling at the paradox we experience when trying to make the most of those last days with a loved one: since you strive to make every moment a quality one, you can end up having some of the best times, ironically, in that saddest of periods, as death waits in the shadows between those picture-perfect trees or behind those giant concrete toadstools like a malevolent leprechaun.

Vicki did her best to keep the party going all the way back to London, bless her, but she was no Jackson, so on the flight home the questions began to gnaw away at me again: what would the next chapter in Mum's story be? When would I hear more news? And what exactly would that news be?

CHAPTER 21

WAITER, THERE'S A TWAT IN MY SOUP

Mum glanced at her watch, then looked up at me across the table to see if I'd noticed her do it. Of course I had. I'd been doing it myself every few minutes for the last hour.

'I should have picked him up on the way. Then I could have hustled him out the door. Sorry, Mum. It's my fault.'

'Don't you dare apologise for him,' she said, stroking my arm, her tone a weary blend of disappointment and maternal coddling.

We were at The Ivy, the plush, Art Deco celebrity haunt in central London. It was hard enough to get a table here at the best of times – and this was the worst of times, it being the Christmas holidays – so keeping the staff waiting for us to order for nearly an hour wasn't making us any friends here, especially since we didn't have faces they would have seen on stage or screen, which nearly every other customer around us appeared to be in smug possession of.

Ruth had booked the table for Mum's birthday lunch. And it was not any old birthday lunch. It was Mum's sixtieth. A momentous occasion for anyone, but one of colossal significance for a woman who'd been looking down the barrel of death for the past year or so. A barrel that had suddenly been shoved right between her eyes.

A month after my holiday to visit them in Vermont, Mum and Ruth had come back to London, where a doctor's appointment had been scheduled immediately for some new tests. I was home alone one evening when the call came. I was washing up, I think, which had become a new pastime of mine (washing up, that is, not thinking – I already did far too much of that), since, living alone, I could no longer blame any festering thing in the kitchen sink on Jake or Will. As I scrubbed the frying pan clean of my blasphemous meal of bacon and egg, I stared out of the window over the industrial landscape of Kings Cross. The winter had drawn in and suddenly everything seemed bleaker, the days were darker, colder. As it does many of us, the changing of the seasons always affected me, and now I struggled more than ever to find a balanced outlook with the added pressure of an imminent update on Mum's condition pushing down on my internal barometer.

Mum had mentioned a slight tummy ache while we were in Vermont, and perhaps I was in denial, but I thought that could be many things, even the after-effects of the operation itself – let's face it, who wouldn't feel a little ache in the abdomen having had half of it ripped out. So when the phone rang and I saw it was Ruth I answered with trepidation, but also with hope.

'The cancer has come back, James,' her voice said in my ear like a ghost. 'More voracious than ever, I'm afraid. Growing faster than even the doctors had expected.'

The cancer has come back, she'd said, as if it was an uninvited house guest, a domestic abuser back from prison. And it was angry now; angry that it had been attacked and banished in the first place, and it was back for revenge, stronger and more determined than ever. My analytical brain knew cancer was simply a non-sentient DNA mutation, but it was easy for my heart to associate human characteristics to something that seemed to act as if it had its own dark will.

I was devastated all over again, lulled into a false sense of security by the good times Mum and I had recently had together, and the apparently unbreakable fortitude I'd witnessed in her. I had assumed we had at least a year or so left, maybe more. I became obsessed with time. Years, months, weeks, days, hours, minutes, even seconds mattered. Consequently Dad's lifelong lack of punctuality was now infuriating.

'What's the plan?' I'd said into the phone looking out at the skeleton of a giant empty gas tower against the Halloween orange of the street-lit city.

'Well,' Ruth explained in business-like tones which attempted to conceal her own breaking heart. 'As is often the case with cancer when it comes back, if the patient decides to go in for a second bout of chemo, it is far less effective. So, if your mum did go for another course, she would probably buy herself a few more months, but at the same time, her quality of life during that period would be reduced considerably by the awful symptoms caused by the chemo itself. Alternatively, if she didn't take the course and enjoyed what time she had left, it would be a shorter time. It's a hell of a decision to make, right?'

Actually, I thought it was a no-brainer. As much as a few months might seem like years to someone on medical death row or to someone like me who now saw a terrible profligacy in the wasting of a single second that could have been spent with a loved one, to spend those few months in pain and sickness caused by the voluntary mainlining of debilitating toxins seemed madness to me. I'd seen the damage done the first time around, and assumed it would be even worse the second time. Selfishly, I remember feeling relieved it was not me having to make the choice, but as it turned out, Mum, and everyone else closest to her, had come to the same conclusion.

She wanted to only spend time with those same people for the final few months and we rallied round her to try to create the most comfortable, nurturing environment possible. Ruth, who had already been acting as her full-time carer, having given up her high-powered city job, dedicated every minute of her life to Mum, as she became increasingly ill. And the fact that Dad couldn't even get his skinny arse here to The Ivy, just for a few hours, on this most special of days, enraged her. She said nothing as we waited. And that was unusual for Ruth. That was how I knew she was fuming. That and her face like thunder – really, really heavy tropical thunder that shakes the very ground you cower on.

Dad had actually been to see Mum a lot recently. Well, a lot more than usual, but with massive gaps between each visit when he'd disappear off the radar completely until I went round and found him in his flat, a little busier, a lot richer, and a little more dishevelled than before. Ruth had graciously invited him to join us for the birthday lunch, and though, since his dalliance with drugs, his poor punctuality had only become worse, we told ourselves he wouldn't possibly screw up something so important as Mum's birthday, especially since it was the last birthday she would probably ever have.

'He'll be here soon.' Mum smiled weakly. 'I don't think even Richard would be late for this one. Now,' she said in an attempt to buoy us all, 'how about a little more champagne?'

Our ever-attentive waiter topped up our glasses – well, mine and Ruth's glasses, and Mum's tippy cup: you know, one of those plastic cups with a spout for toddlers or the disabled. Since her coordination had deteriorated further Ruth had bought this for Mum.

'Look what I have to use now, because I'm such a klutz!' she had said, blushing, the first time I'd seen her using it.

We had laughed then, but I'd had to stifle the tears too, just as I did now seeing her drink out of moulded plastic in the crystal-glass-tinkling, silver-clinking surroundings of this most luxurious and exclusive of eateries, dressed in unusually loose and flowing clothes to cover the bulges the steroids had dumped on her, her hair short after recently growing back, but growing back grey to add insult to injury.

A wave of frustration competed with the booze for pride of place in my veins and I reached in my pocket for my car keys. *I'll go round there right now and drag him out of that fucking drug den by the scruff of his poxy tank top if I find him there. I'll drag him all the way here and make him kiss Mum's feet in front of the assembled glitterati so they can all make a mental note to channel that scene as they prepare for a role in the next Hollywood blockbuster.* But I didn't, of course. It was miles away and hours in London traffic to Limehouse and back, and it was bad enough him not being here, let alone me leaving Mum too, however perversely noble my intentions. Instead my fingers just caressed the keyring my car keys were on; the keyring with a football motif engraved on it; the keyring Mum had presented to me on my last birthday in a light blue Tiffany box; a classically boyish present from Mummy to her little soldier, I had thought, until I saw the note on the card nestled in the box beside the present which read:

Darling James, Carry this wherever you go and I'll be with you always. Love Mum xx

And suddenly the little trinket gained an emotional weight that was hard for me to bear. As we'd hugged wordlessly in the kitchen it felt like the first 'goodbye', the acknowledgement that there was not that much time left now, that we needed to start getting into that finite frame of mind. But how was it possible to accept that this was the final birthday gift I would ever receive from my mother?

An hour and half after the time our table was booked for, Dad scurried in and sat down, looking fragile, to say the least, probably on a huge downer after a hard night on the meth.

'I'm sorry, so sorry. I got caught up with a client and then the traffic was—'

'Give it a rest, Dad!' I hissed contemptuously. 'We've heard it all before.'

'What? I had to—'

'Enough with the excuses, Dad. There are no excuses for this one.' *Except for being a drug addict*, I almost added but decided to keep that, as I had about most of Dad's recent life choices, to myself.

'Yes, yes, you're right,' he conceded. 'It's not about me today, is it,' he said, raising a glass of water. 'Marilyn, many happy return—'

We all cringed.

He coughed with a phlegmy violence which turned some star-coiffed heads. 'Excuse me. Happy birthday, Marilyn.'

We all toasted Mum, of course, but resented the toastmaster swanning in so massively late and so massively tactless. And being such a massive twat!

Ruth could barely look at him throughout the remainder of the meal, and I chewed with a lemon face on the wilted idea I'd always harboured that Dad was the one person I would be able to rely on if Mum was ever diagnosed with a terminal illness. He was supposed to be my comfort, my rock, the one who would tell me it was all OK, my protector... just a normal bloody parent, for God's sake! And my only remaining one. But he was such a bloody mess that he was the one who needed worrying about, taking care of, while I was the one who had to be the rock, the parent. But I was just the child, wasn't I? That was all I wanted to be anyway. I suppose I'd never dreamt there would be a time when I would have to be anything else.

CHAPTER 22

GOING SOUTH

Did the security guard outside Ruth's apartment block just give me a look of commiseration rather than his usual rancid-curry fart-smeller's face? No, he couldn't have, that surely wasn't in his repertoire of expressions – well, I'd certainly never seen it before anyway, and I wished I hadn't now, as it only served to rub my nose in the idea that I was losing someone.

Mel C was jumping into the back of a chauffeur-driven Audi as we approached the building, and she gave Vicki and me a quick wave, her usual gold-toothed smile concealed behind lips which appeared to me to make a warm *Chin-up, mate!* sort of shape. But perhaps I just imagined it.

We were on our way to Ruth's place for Mum's second birthday party. The lunch at The Ivy wasn't technically on her birthday so we had another gathering on the day itself, 30 December – call her greedy but let's let her off, all thing

considered, eh? Mum felt she had a lot to celebrate. The cancer
– that manipulative little homewrecker – had made the insidious
and calculated decision to move into multiple parts of her body,
and was greedily eating away at it now, every moment of every
day. This – you won't be surprised to hear – was not why Mum
felt she had a lot to celebrate. She was celebrating the fact that,
despite the intruder, she was still remarkably able.

If it wasn't for all those pitying faces on the people we passed
on our way here (even the bloke in the off licence handed me
my change mournfully – unless it was my choice of Merlot he
was lamenting), I might not have noticed the way Mum walked
from the kitchen to greet us. The limp was slight, but a limp
nevertheless. Her hand butterflied around her back, ready to
clutch it should the pain shoot through again. She was still
herself – the same smile she'd always had, the same warmth in
the hug she gave me – but she was much slower now: a vision
of mortality, though she was doing all she could to make us still
doubt the end was near.

'I've made it!' she said with all the triumph of an Everest
conqueror watching an avalanche hurtle towards them. 'I've
reached sixty!'

That comment caught me unawares. In the back of my mind
I was thinking that this was the least we should have hoped for.
The doctors originally suggested she would have two and half
years, and we'd only had one, for Christ's sake! So this wasn't an
achievement at all, it was a let-down, a failure. We were owed a

year at least. And I didn't care who was going to cough up – Life, Death, God, Bupa – someone had to give us our due.

I didn't say any of this out loud, of course. I just hugged her as hard as I could without causing her more pain and said, 'Happy birthday, Mum!'

Dad had been invited to this party too, despite his awful yet predictable display of tardiness at the lunch. So I was nearly incontinent with shock when he arrived only fifteen minutes late. But this time he was not his usual chatty self. Perhaps, I thought, that was simply because he didn't need to regale us with a thousand invented excuses on arrival, since he was basically on time on this occasion. But it wasn't that. Throughout the party he sat in the corner like a lamp with a blown fuse. Sadness was seeping out of his pores. He must have run out of whatever anti-anguish roll-on he'd been using for the past year or so. He could no longer mask the effect Mum's imminent loss was having on him.

'I'm losing my rock, son,' he said confidentially when we found ourselves alone for a moment in the kitchen. 'I know we haven't been together for some time. And we could never be together, ultimately, it was always destined not to be, what with us both being...' He hesitated.

'Gay,' I said promptly, to show that it didn't make me feel any less of a human being to have been conceived by two homosexuals – not anymore anyway.

'Mmm. But your mum is still the love of my life. Always will be.'

I made a mental note to forgive him when he was next late for something – as long as it was less than one hour late.

The festive season was over too quickly, as ever, and I went back to work, a few pounds heavier with food and booze and a whole lot heavier in my heart. Mum's condition hung over me like a black cloud now. I was waiting for some awful news, the next step in the inexorable downward spiral of her health. I spent hours wondering how it would actually happen: how would her body react? What would that bastard cancer do next? My morbid curiosity was overpowering – how does someone actually die from cancer? Google was there, as ever, to inform and depress me further.

I continued to see Mum every other day usually, and while there were a few signs of further deterioration in her condition, time with her was still strangely normal, almost as it would have been if there was no illness at all. Then, one seemingly run-of-the-mill day at work in April, I received a call from Ruth. She told me that overnight, things had 'gone south' with Mum, and that I probably should come over, as long as there was nothing too pressing at work. *As long as there was nothing too pressing at work?* As if I was going to prioritise the Heinz Baked Beans account over my mum now that Ruth had called and told me things had *gone south*. And what the fuck did gone south mean anyway? Gone south was what birds do in the winter, not mums. Gone south was what my ball sack had been doing at an alarming rate since I'd surmounted the hill of thirty and was dry tobogganing at great speed down into the valley of middle age. Apart from her weird insinuation that Mum was emigrating, Ruth also said something about Mum's state of mind being somehow the problem. That made no sense to me – I'd only seen her a couple of days ago and she was completely compos mentis then. I chewed this over like a piping-hot chip as I ran down Oxford Street for the tube, having excused myself from work, noting the high level of relief I felt to be getting out of the office – that shouldn't be right, I thought, especially under the circumstances! But it was just an indication of how deep in a rut I already was in my work, despite that work being at the highly reputed digital marketing agency Six & Co. The other apparently inappropriate feeling I had as I shot underground towards Hampstead was that morbid curiosity to see the next stage of the disease. What would I find when I got to the flat? The anticipation was almost too much to bear.

On the walk up the steep hill from Hampstead tube station to Ruth's flat I was breathless with 'what ifs'. What if Mum is close to death? What if I can't cope with her worsened state of health? What if I somehow fail in my duties as an only son helping to care for my dying mother? What if this is actually *it*? What if I'm about to witness *the end*?

Ruth greeted me at the door looking tired and ashen. She led me to the spare room, which now doubled as a makeshift medical room – one of Mum's wishes was to see out her last months in the comfort of her home, rather than a hospice, and this was thankfully being fulfilled.

And then I saw her. She was sitting up in bed with her eyes closed, and initially I didn't really see an obvious issue. Maybe she was just feeling particularly rough today? That's how it goes with this thing, isn't it? You have your good days and your bad days. It doesn't mean you've gone south for good. Just like the birds for the winter perhaps, but not for good. Not forever. Spring was just around the corner. Despite the morning of snow we'd had earlier in the month and the kind of temperatures that were fooling me into believing my scrotum was tightening up again permanently, May was just days away – the month of frolicking lambs, morris dancing and blossoming trees. The time of rebirth. Everything was going to be all right, wasn't it?

Ruth spoke first. 'Hey! Your son is here to see you.'

Mum opened her eyes and looked over at me. 'Oh, hello, darling.'

'Hi, Mum. You OK?'

Apart from the fact that she seemed a little surprised to see me, she sounded fine. You see! Nothing to worry about.

And then, without warning, she closed her eyes and appeared to nod off.

I immediately looked back at Ruth quizzically, searching for an explanation. But she could only return a sad, helpless expression.

Then, equally as sudden, Mum opened her eyes, looked up and saw me again. 'Hello, darling!' She chirped, almost a carbon copy of what she'd said and done seconds before.

Now I was starting to understand why I needed to be here. But what did this strange behaviour have to do with *ovarian* cancer? I knew things could 'go south' at any point now, but I was expecting something in her body to fail near the vicinity of where it all started – in the southern regions in fact. Her head was miles north of her ovaries. The confusion was frustrating me. Where the fuck was the doctor?

We stayed with Mum, waiting for his arrival. She kept repeating the bizarre pattern – one minute she was wide-eyed, alert, talking completely normally; the next she was unconscious, lights off, nobody home. And each time she did wake up, she had completely forgotten the previous conversation.

My first instinct was to call Dad. I wasn't even sure if he'd pick up given his recent behaviour – increasingly erratic, even more unreliable than usual – but I dialled anyway. To my surprise he answered straightaway. I quickly tried to describe Mum's situation, convey the lack of coherence she was displaying. Dad fired off a few quick questions and, despite the lack of detail I could offer, he seemed to comprehend the seriousness of the change in her condition.

'I'll be there as soon as I can.'

'OK, Dad.'

'Erm… in a few hours.'

That's as soon as you can?

I sighed, too drained to argue, 'OK, Dad.'

My frustration with him was relieved by the doctor's arrival: at last we'd have some answers. He did the check-up, then took us outside the room to deliver the news. We both steeled ourselves for the worst – it was becoming a familiar process.

'She has developed a bleed on the brain,' he stated, 'caused by the brain tumour that travelled up from her body and established itself in her head. The bleed has caused brain damage, quite severe brain damage, I should add, which will only worsen over time.'

'What does that mean for her?' Ruth was clearly distraught at the news, but tried to keep it together.

'It means she has a matter of days now,' the doctor said in a tone that achieved the perfect balance of empathy, sympathy and clinical descriptiveness, somehow conveying the idea that at least my mother would soon be free from her suffering.

So that was it – the final bombshell. This really was the end-phase. I was soon to experience the death of my mum, someone who raised me, loved me unconditionally (no matter how much of a little shit I was on regular occasions), arguably the person who would love me more than anyone else I would ever meet in my life.

As soon as the doctor left, Ruth and I hugged, tears flowing. And not for the first time, amongst the myriad thoughts that were running through my head, I contemplated the fact that my anchor, my support, wasn't my own father, the person I always expected to be there during a crisis such as this, but instead it was someone I didn't even know seven years ago, a relative stranger with whom I had become so close over these last few years. This sent a pang of resentment towards Dad shooting through me; resentment towards someone who was going off the rails at the worst time possible. But it also made me even more grateful that Ruth had come into our lives – she was a gift.

Soon after the doctor left, Dad arrived. He looked familiarly dishevelled – like a proper meth head – and that pang of resentment pierced me again. Nevertheless, Ruth and I sensitively shared the diagnosis.

He listened intently. Then took off his glasses and, as if they were the thing keeping his face together, his expression crumpled. And he cried.

I had only seen him cry once before: when I was twelve and his own mother had died. It was shocking then for a boy to see a normally stoic father figure break down like that, and I never forgot it. This time, after what he had said at Mum's sixtieth, I think I expected it. Every time I saw him he looked more and more like that painting Karol had done of him – his physical frailty a reflection of his emotional frailty. Now he looked utterly broken. Utterly depressed. Ruth gave us some time together in the room with Mum and she continued her bizarre pattern of waking up, saying hi in a slightly confused what-are-you-doing-here? kind of way, then falling back to sleep. I watched Dad as he desperately tried to have a normal conversation with her, every time being cut short as she dropped off, like having a mobile phone call with someone in an area with really bad reception – bloody frustrating.

He turned and looked at me, bereft.

'How long has she been like this?' he asked, almost pleading.

'Since this morning,' I said with a certain authority which slapped me in the face, because here was my own Dad asking me for answers on Mum. The little boy inside me wanted *him* to have all the answers; I wanted to be the one asking the questions. That was when I broke down and sank into a chair. Dad stayed in his, consumed by his own grief, unable to reach out, barely in a state to look after himself, let alone his own son.

CHAPTER 23
THE DRUGS DON'T WORK

For the next few days I camped out at Mum and Ruth's place, my emotional tent buffeted by a whirlwind of visits – visits from relatives, close friends, not-so-close friends, randoms I didn't even know, doctors and palliative nurses, who floated through the storm like angels lighting the way: cuddly, cardiganed oases of calm and control in these tempestuous times. There were so many people toing and froing, in fact, that this place of dying felt more like a house party, a never-ending house party – it was even, strangely, less depressing than some house parties I'd propped up the kitchen sink at over the years. There were even, like at all good house parties, plenty of drugs involved, except there was only one person on them, and she was lying in the spare room hooked up to a heart monitor.

Mum was now unable to communicate properly and was unable to walk, yet when she had those moments of waking up, she would try and get herself out of bed. If we'd let her do this she would have ended up in a heap on the floor. So you can see the house party comparison persisted – this indeed could have been, and was, Jake, Will or me at various points in recent messy times. But here the comparison ended with a series of heart-wrenching tussles.

It was decided by the doctors, since we had no idea how much pain she was in, to up Mum's morphine. But frustratingly, every time we increased it, she still seemed to be waking up and trying to get out of bed in a confused state. So much so that I had to sit on the bed repeatedly and hold her down with all my strength to keep her from falling out. It was traumatic – for her and for me – a nightmarish way for Mum to leave this life. She couldn't understand why we were doing it. She even shouted out at one point, 'Why?' just as she'd done countless times when frustrated with something me or Dad had done, something inane like leaving crumbs on the sofa or forgetting to do the washing up, but this time there was a tortured anguish in her tone that was unbearable, and that reminder of a life when death was something that happened to other people, and family was an unbreakable unit, twisted the knife even more for me. It hurt at first, then it made me angry.

'Why can't someone fucking sort this out? This shouldn't be happening!' I thought during one of those episodes, feeling like I'd been press-ganged into some secret suburban ring that got off on mum wrestling.

Mum's best friend, Dawn, came into the room to help just then.

'I'm sorry you have to see her like this,' I said, my voice trembling with the struggle and emotion.

But Dawn's response was an unexpected scolding. 'Oh, don't you apologise to me, James! Me and your Mum go back years, this is what friendship is all about.'

Fuck! Is it? Up until then I'd thought friendship was all about getting basted with Jake and Will and bragging to each other (or lying in my case) about how many girls we'd shagged, taking the piss out of each other's failures and celebrating Arsenal winning the double. Sheesh! There was so much more to this growing up business than I had been led to believe when I signed up for life on Earth.

Eventually, the nurses found the right dose. Along with my relief – euphoria almost, when Mum was finally peacefully asleep and free from pain – was a flash of pride that my Mum was so kick-arse that she wasn't going down until you gave her enough morphine to sedate a horse. And then, as I relived those moments when she was struggling to stay awake and to get up, the terrible notion came to me that I'd just had the final two-way interaction I would ever have with her, and such a mangled, combative interaction it had been. But both Ruth and I could not deny that sense of relief as things calmed down and we could prepare ourselves for the final moment in the way we felt it should be – in quiet, hushed tones and slow movements.

One night I asked the nurse who was taking over to sit with Mum as we got some sleep whether I should be worried about the gurgling sound coming from Mum's throat.

'Nothing to worry about,' she cooed soothingly. 'It's just mucus that collects in the airways when someone is close to the end. You may have heard the phrase *the death rattle*?'

I nodded.

'That's what it means.'

That is not a sound you ever want to hear, trust me, but at least it was another sign that it would all be over for Mum soon. And yes, I admit it, over for me too. It could be a day or hours, but it was coming.

I went to my bed on the sofa in the living room and felt like I had only slept for a minute when I heard Ruth's urgent whisper easily cutting through the dark stillness of the early spring morning.

'James. I think your mum's going.'

I was out of bed in a millisecond, immediately alert, the adrenaline pumping. 'How could Ruth tell?' was all I could think as I hurried to Mum's room.

'She called out to me, James. I think she knew she was about to go. I can't see if she's breathing.'

That hideous death rattle had not been a constant feature for Mum, thankfully, but that meant it was even more difficult to tell when her breathing finally stopped.

Ruth put her ear to Mum's mouth. She looked up, unsure. So I put my ear to Mum's mouth too. My turn to look unsure. How the hell do these paramedics ever know what to do?

'I can't feel anything.'

'Me neither.'

'But her breath could be just really shallow, right?'

'Yeah.'

The nurse having gone, we looked around the room hopelessly, looking for assistance. The shelves of bookshops these days were groaning under the weight of all the *How To Look After Your Newborn Baby* books on them, but where was just one *How To Know When Your Mum Has Finally Popped Off* book when you needed it?

I rifled through mental drawers full of memorised scenes from my favourite TV shows. *What would Captain Kirk do in this situation? Get Dr McCoy to hover his tricorder over the body and diagnose everything you could possibly imagine in a nanosecond, of course! OK, perhaps we need a slightly less futuristic example then. What would Gandalf do in this situation? Wave his magic staff about and contact the elves who would ship Mum off to Valinor. OK, perhaps we need a slightly more contemporary example then. Think! Think!* It was at times like these in the past – not that there were any times in the past when I was trying to deduce whether my mum had passed away or not, but there were plenty of times where I was lost for answers – that Dad would be the one I would go to and he'd always have an answer, words that sounded steeped in the wisdom of experience, even if they were not really based in any scientific fact at all. But that wasn't really an option now, was it, since Dad would be too busy self-destructing, lighting up meth pipes and racking up lines on mirrors like a fucking teenager—

'A mirror!' I blurted out, like Sherlock Holmes or something, and Watson hurried off to get her compact from the other room.

When she returned she put it to Mum's mouth. We looked for any signs of condensation.

Nothing.

And then I just came out with it. 'You realise Mum would have found this hilarious.' I spoke about her in the past tense, as a person no longer with us.

We both knew it was over.

And Ruth laughed, a normal laugh, enjoying the black comedy of it all too, because if there was one type of humour Mum always reacted to it was the very dark, morbid type. I was amazed we were both laughing, with my still-warm, dead mother lying in front of us, but it felt like a victory in the face of such hopeless sadness. I lost count of how many times we hugged, in grief, or with relief, but I remember distinctly the time during which Ruth bawled, 'I love you, son.' She was hysterical with emotion, but I knew she meant it, and it meant the world to me. At a time when the two major mainstays of my world were either gone or floundering, our bond had strengthened by the day, we had grown to rely on each other emotionally, and I was more than ready to accept her as a surrogate parent, so very different from the surviving biological one, but that's precisely why I knew… well, I couldn't *know* for sure, not amid the fog of death we stood in, but at least I *believed* she would always be there for me, as I would be for her.

Just then, that floundering mainstay of my world tumbled into the apartment.

'How is she?'

'She's gone, Dad.'

'Oh, no.'

That was all he said. Oh, no. And what else was there to say? And yet in that little phrase there was so much meaning: 'Oh, no, I was going to be here an hour ago,' which I later found out was the case, but of course he was late. 'Oh, no, it happened again.' You see, when he was on his way to see his own mum, who was in her death throes in hospital, also wracked with cancer, he turned back home having realised he'd forgotten to turn on the intruder alarm – therefore reaching the hospital just moments after she passed. And perhaps the most poignant of all: 'Oh, no, what am I going to do without her?' Because though he had been without her in a sense since they had split up just over a decade ago, she had always been there for him, always been that rock he described her as on her sixtieth, always been the soft, supportive voice on the end of the phone.

You didn't seem to miss her much when you were bouncing off the walls of sweaty nightclubs, I thought, during one of those angry moments that pepper grief. And then during one of those more palatable philosophical moments I reckoned that perhaps it was enough for him just to know she was there; he could always call on her if needed, like a boy running back to his mummy for reassurance whenever things got too much. A bit like I did.

Friends and family were duly called and filed into the apartment to pay their respects. One of my oldest friends,

Elliot, was among them and I showed him in to view Mum's body with a bizarre detachment, already convinced as I was that this vessel was just something that looked a bit like Mum; sure it was no longer really her.

'Touch her!' I said to him. 'I've never felt a dead body before. Have you?'

'No, I haven't,' he said, looking at me incredulously, his nose scrunched up, perhaps at the clinical odour in the room, or more likely at my weird suggestion. 'Nah, I'll give it a miss, if you don't mind.'

I nonchalantly took Mum's hand. The fingers were curled up. I tried to uncurl them. Rigor mortis had set in and they were stuck fast. But even this didn't faze me. There was so much relief associated with her death, if I'm honest, that her body really had little emotional impact on me.

As Elliot scampered out of the bedroom back to the safety of the appropriately named living room, Ruth handed me a letter. It was from Mum. And as I read it, all my cool indifference around her body melted into hot, visceral emotion as I heard her voice again, felt her spirit. In those words she had written, she had come back to life for a little while, talking to me from beyond the grave. It must have been as hard for her to write it, knowing what was coming, as it was for me to read it, but it was a real gift. I admired her for having the courage to write it and I held on to the words for dear life over the following months as the winds of mourning blasted me.

To my darling James,

Without wishing to make you sadder than you already are, I want to share some of my feelings with you.

I wonder if you know how much I have always loved and adored you. I know that sometimes, as a mother, I didn't always cover myself with glory, and for that I have never forgiven myself. But I tried to be the very best mum that I could be, and I hope you have some good memories of your childhood.

Watching you grow & develop into the person you are now has been a source of joy and admiration. You have made some good friends and that is because you yourself are such a good friend, loyal, funny and always there for people. I watch with amazement your confidence, always ready to face a challenge and take on new things.

Didn't we have a wonderful time in Provence? And Vermont. I am so grateful to have been given that time to spend with you.

I hate to leave you. I wish I could have stayed around for you, to see what happened in your life. But I know you will do whatever you choose to do. My prayer is that you are happy. That is what I want for you, happiness and a sense of fulfilment throughout your life.

I love you so much, my lovely handsome son. Just know that whatever you do, wherever you go, I will always occupy a corner of your heart. Be proud and know how much pride and happiness you gave to your old mum.

I love you xxx

I'm not sure who the confident, handsome, funny guy she was talking about in the letter was, but perhaps, with all the extra-sensory perception that mothers seem to have when it comes to their little soldiers, she could see something in me that I couldn't, at least not yet.

Those days of frolicking lambs, dancing round the maypole, blossom and rebirth passed me by, I'm afraid. Dad disappeared off the radar completely, no doubt diving even deeper into the comfortably numbing waters of his drug addiction, while I merely listened to 'Comfortably Numb' by Roger Waters (and Dave Gilmour, of course). The funeral came around soon enough and, like every significant event in our family life, I was tense, anticipating whether Dad would turn up on time or even at all.

So Ruth and I hatched a foolproof plan to make sure he not only made an appearance but made a prompt one: we arranged that he would pick me up on the way to the funeral, assuming that there was no way he would allow himself to be the reason his only son missed his mother's funeral.

What were we smoking?! Something far more dopey than whatever Dad was, if we thought that was going to somehow change the habit of a lifetime. Oh, he did pick me up all right, but he was excruciatingly late and so when we got to the cemetery the entire congregation was waiting for us, looking at us, focused on our atrocious lack of punctuality instead of reflecting on my mother and her life. I've never been so embarrassed. This was a whole other league and genre of embarrassment to walking in on your father's heavily occupied sex room, or even being screamed at by Sasithorn Sonjohnkoksoong in the middle of a packed student union bar – and given your average person's screaming was her default speaking voice, you can imagine how embarrassing that was. I was furious at Dad. How dare he put me in that position? I know he was devastated by Mum's death too, but right then he just seemed to care more about himself than anyone else.

Susan and her family in L.A. didn't even come to the funeral. As Dad descended into dealing and addiction, his contact with her had decreased, to the point that he stopped returning her calls. Susan would call me a number of times expressing her concern, and not really understanding the situation. She wondered if she'd offended him in some way. I tried to explain that he was a hopeless addict, utterly dysfunctional, but no matter how many similar people she'd coached through therapy, Susan found this apparent rejection by Dad very hard to take.

As I watched Mum's casket lowered into the earth, idioms concerning nails in coffins kept rising with the steamy sadness inside me. Dad's behaviour today should have been the final nail as far as he and I were concerned, but imminent events were about to propel me back closer to him and his self-destructive lifestyle than I could ever have imagined.

CHAPTER 24

SABOTAGE

Vicki had been by my side throughout Mum's death and the period of mourning that followed, at least in spirit if not always in body – after all, she had a job and a family and a life of her own to deal with too. But if I haven't mentioned her much over the last few pages it was because I probably took her support and presence a little bit for granted – OK, a lot – and I guess there's only so much of that someone can take before needing some time for themselves, which is exactly what Vicki took when she went away on a little holiday a couple of months after Mum's death.

When she got back I was eager to see her, to tell her how shit work was, how shit Dad was being, how shit life in general was, but she said she was ill and could I leave it for a bit. No problem, I told her, and got on with having a load more shit times so I could regale her with them when next we met. When the time came, however, it was her who needed to speak to me, she said. What could she possibly have to speak to me about that was more important than my telling her how shit things were?

'I had a... erm... bit of a fling while I was away,' she said through her tears. 'Just a fling, nothing more. But it made me realise that you and me' – she took a deep breath to try and steady herself – 'we're just not right for each other anymore.'

My first broken heart. Stomping with big dog-shit covered boots all over the carpet of my life so recently stained with my first family loss – assuming I held carpets dear. Which I didn't. My flat didn't even have carpets. It had that easy to clean wood-effect lino. But anyway, you get the idea, especially if you're partial to your own shagpile. I was shattered. I begged Vicki to give us another chance, feeling the sense of impending loss more acutely than I might have done had my mum not recently passed away. Vicki was distraught too. She had really invested a lot in me and my family. Remember that surprise Scalextric party I told you about in Chapter One? Vicki had organised that for me, and when Dad – you guessed it – failed to turn up with the excuse that he had been so engrossed in YouTube he had lost track of time, she was the one that laid into him about it, not me – for me that was becoming all too normal.

So we gave it another try, for five minutes, but it was clear we were flogging a dead horse. And so I did what so many blokes do to prove to the world that they're so over the ex – especially an ex who had a fling – just a fling, mind you, nothing more – not that that bothered me in the FUCKING LEAST. Yes, whilst the female stereotypes of the world cried into large vats of Ben and Jerry's and slagged off their exes to their long-suffering best friends, this male stereotype went straight out and hooked up with a new girl. Kate. And when I say, *went straight out and hooked up*, I mean, of course, I got back on Jdate.com and after a huge amount of time stumbling and stuttering through various failed attempts to coax a suitable rebound to the first date stage, I managed to bag a drink with Kate.

I suggested we meet at an oriental fusion restaurant called Inamo round the corner from my offices in Soho. It was a space-age place with interactive menus projected onto your tabletop. It appealed to the nerd that would always be so deeply ensconced in me and I thought it would be a good ice-breaker. So after another generally unrewarding day at work I bounced out of the office looking forward to a bit of good food, and to meeting Kate, of course.

Kate looked very much like her photograph − always a bonus, especially since she looked attractive in her photo. And as I got my geek on and explained the finer points of the technology behind interactive menus to Kate, she giggled and happily prodded the projections on the table before her. She listened. Not just to my futuristic waffle but to everything I had to say. If I was to rewrite her dating profile for her I would put, nurturing, caring, sensitive and attractive. Any other time in the past I would have translated such a profile as: stalker, frumpy, unhinged and plain. But right then nurturing, caring and sensitive was exactly what I needed – in other words, someone, in my newly motherless state, who would mother me.

Incredibly, she agreed to another date, but as we parted ways I wasn't skipping down the road, I was just bloody relieved. The second date led to another, and before long we were an item. I even started staying at her place outside London, which meant I had to commute all the way in with the rest of the drably suited, po-faced umbrella mob pressing up against each other in ways that in any other situation would be called sexual harassment; each of them sneering their quiet indignity to their Kindles or papers at everyone else's audacity in travelling to work at the same time as them. Even when I was waking up in Kings Cross, where my commute could only be shorter if I slept on the office floor, I would wake with the stomach of a rollercoaster rider – a rider who had vertigo and had eaten too many burgers before the ride. Now this additional effort to get in to work just added to the sense of dread I felt about the job and began to depress me about staying over at Kate's.

The more Kate was nurturing, the more I would catch her profile out of the corner of my eye and write plain where I once wrote attractive. The more she was sensitive, the more our long, peaceful drives where we didn't need to pollute the air with wasteful words became marathons of awkward silence. The more she was caring, the more her night-time nasal purring morphed into fucking irritating and thunderous snoring.

In my unhealthily needy and confused emotional state, Kate's snoring became a level of aural assault I had not yet experienced in my so far somnolent nights on Earth. So much so that surreptitiously I invested in a set of earplugs and slipped them in with secret agent stealth whenever Kate dropped off.

The plugs helped a lot, but there was no plug to mask the way her breath now began to repulse me when I went in for a kiss. Poor Kate! I'd never had a problem with her breath before. Perhaps what was really repulsing me was the idea that she was just an emotional crutch for me, a safety blanket and more of a convenience than anything else. Whatever the reason, there was no denying it, I was going off her. And perhaps that was why I invited her round to my dad's flat.

'He'd love to meet you.'

'It'll be nice to meet him too. I've heard so much about him,' Kate beamed.

Of course, she hadn't heard the half of it and her jaw dropped to cartoon depths as I introduced her to all the familiar faces waiting on Dad's couch to be admitted to his office for their fix; as I showed her round the seedy flat and told her to pop her head into the sex room, which was happily home to some head-popping of its own at the time. Her eyes now the things doing the popping, I crowned the tour with an introduction to Dad, who was too busy shovelling measures from a huge pile of white powder to engage in pleasantries with some girl I'd just met and brought here, potentially jeopardising the security of his den of iniquity.

Kate made her excuses and left. And just as my sabotaging self had designed it, I never saw her again.

Without the slightest pang of regret I enjoyed my short walk to work the next day from my own flat in Kings Cross – a small consolation for having to go to work at all.

My gosh, I thought, Dad has probably got this life thing better sussed than I gave him credit for. His commute is from his bedroom to his living room. And he answers to no one but himself.

'James, could I see you for a moment?'

The bloke I had to answer to, the Director of Client Services, called me into his office. If my guts could sink any further, they would be seeping out from beneath my little toe nails right now.

'James.'

'Yes?'

'Erm. Well, you'll recall that at our last review there were some concerns with your performance,' the director said, 'and I'm afraid we've just seen no improvement over the last few months and so… we're going to have to let you go. With immediate effect.'

It was a kick in the nuts of such force, I was floored. Me? Grade A student, high achiever, diligent worker, sacked? But that was just it. I had lost all my diligence and focus at work what with everything that had been happening over the past few years. And finally my negligence was racing up behind me with rabid jaws ready to take a chunk out of my skinny arse.

'Hang on! Hang the fuck on! You know I've been through some personal shit recently, but besides that, I don't think I've been given a fair chance here. The kind of accounts you have provided me with recently are hardly the kind of accounts someone can show their true potential with. In fact, it wouldn't surprise me if you had given me such duff accounts in order to make it easier for you to get rid of me, which let's face it is what you've wanted to do for ages.'

I was ranting. Me? Calm, shy, dependable James, ranting? Yes. And I wasn't merely ranting, I was throwing my toys, dummy *and* diarrhoea-covered nappy out of the pram in a manner which in hindsight was terrifyingly reminiscent of one of Dad's recent tantrums. Needless to say, it didn't help me hold on to my job. I sloped out of the office a few excruciating 'clearing my desk' minutes later, into a sunny, warm day, and while the immediate worry was where my next source of income was going to come from, I was surprised to find I suddenly felt brighter, more energised, even more confident. I called up Jake and laughed about it down the phone.

'Yeah, but if there was ever a good time to get sacked, this is it, mate,' I smiled.

'How do you work that out?'

'Well, now I can watch the Ashes in full, uninterrupted. This is going to be a great summer.' I grinned, though I think Jake was just as unconvinced by me as I was.

CHAPTER 25

THE GAME

Summer 2009. Rain stopped play frequently and consequently interrupted my uninterrupted coverage of the Ashes. So I went to the cinema to catch the latest Marvel movie or had my head in the PlayStation trying to distract myself from the truth: my pride was so dented from being sacked and dumped that I was considering taking it in to a panel beater; my mum was gone, my dad going. Yes, rain really had stopped play. Like any self-respecting nerd, my laptop was always there to shield me from reality and I'd while away my days on the dole in cyberspace, but not by playing internet video games or in chat rooms debating which captain was the best the USS *Enterprise* had ever had. No! This nerd was getting his geek on in order to undertake his biggest marketing campaign to date: selling myself. Oh no, I wasn't looking for a new job. I was looking for ladies... Well, to be honest, one perfect lady. I felt terrible about the way things had gone with Kate, the way I had basically used her, but that experience had not put me off the dating game; it had fired me up to get it right this time. I was on a mission, not to shag as many girls as possible (yes, really! The whole one-night-stand thing still scared the life out of me), but to find The One. And since I had nothing better to do, it became my full-time job. Some psychologists might say I was looking for a new family in the wake of the disintegration of my former one, and they may well be right. All I knew, since Mum died, was that life was short and I wasn't getting any younger, so I threw everything at it. What did I have to lose?

I soon unearthed this theory known as The Game. There was a book on it, and I immediately went out and bought it – as well as a large intellectual-looking political biography so I could hide the dating book underneath it at the checkout. The shop assistant's smirk as she examined the book, ostensibly for its barcode, told me I had failed miserably there. Anyway, the premise of the book, which I tore into the moment I got home, was that, based on how you acted, your body language, what you said and how you said it, you could dramatically improve your success rate with women. I bloody hoped that was true. There was even a reality TV show where some expert Casanova-type taught a group of desperate – I mean, eager – young men the ways of The Game. Each episode, they had to complete a challenge such as: walk into a nightclub and pull a complete stranger. I was hooked and soaked up every tip and technique as ravenously as I consumed the Chinese food I had delivered to the door – no time to cook. I discovered there were entire courses you could sign up to, videos you could watch, even email templates you could download that were designed to improve your reply hit rate. It seemed too good to be true. Nevertheless I spent hours, days lapping it up, taking notes, crafting emails, watching tutorials. If only I had been so diligent with my media degree I would have been the head of a Hollywood mega studio by now – well, why not? I already had the prerequisite Jewish blood coursing through my veins.

After finally sending the first batch of emails I was so shocked to find my inbox quickly filling with replies that I nearly spilt scolding wonton soup in my crotch and ended my new life as a stud muffin before it had even begun. And within a couple of email exchanges, as promised by the dating gurus, I was bagging the phone number of each woman. However that meant, of course, I actually had to speak to them now with my very own voice – The Game could have most definitely been up in seconds. But I followed the instructions of the online mentors, kept the calls brief so they didn't have time to suss out that there was a quivering wreck hiding beneath the sound of the head-tossing, leg-spread Lothario who came out with lines like, 'I'm warning you, if you have two heads I'm walking straight back out that bar. Ha, ha!' and before I knew it I had more dates per week than you've had hot dinners – and me too, judging by all those cold, half-eaten takeaway trays lying around the flat.

When it came to the actual date itself, there were more nuggets to help me through from that Open University of

Wooing I'd been attending so studiously, and incredibly they worked, even though the women were now sitting in front of the physical antithesis of the Don Juan they'd heard on the phone and read online. I felt like such a playboy as I left each bar after another successful date. I was buzzing. And more often than not I wanted to keep that buzz going and one easy way to do that was visit Dad and spark up a meth pipe. 'Fuck it!' I thought. 'You only live once. Besides, it's not like I have to get up for work in the morning, is it.' And by popping in on Dad occasionally I could keep an eye on him, I told myself; maximise my time with the old man, who, like me, wasn't getting any younger. In fact he was looking more fragile by the day.

Popping in occasionally soon became popping in frequently, which very quickly became virtually living in Dad's flat. At some point I had made an unconscious decision to make it my new home from home, even though I still had the Kings Cross flat – that wasn't in jeopardy due to my lack of income because, as you will recall, Dad was my landlord and he was going very easy on me in my time of need. And now, as he reached into a large Tupperware box in the bottom of one of his filing cabinets and offered me two grand in fifty-quid notes, he told me not to worry about money until I was back on my feet. I know what you're thinking: 'If I were unemployed I would be inclined to move in with the dad who threw thousands of pounds at me on a regular basis too.' But it really wasn't the main motivation. Although it was little more than a drugs den and potentially a dangerous place to hang out in more ways than one, Dad's flat represented a sense of safety for me; it was comforting being there; it was the closest thing I had left to a family home... And there was loads of free crystal meth, of course, or 'ice', as it was also known. In fact, it had many names, so many it was hard to keep up and caused me no end of worry that Dad had branched out into pimping out young women when I heard someone ask, 'How much for a bit of Tina?' Until they pointed out that crystal = Christine = Tina, get it? I was always half in awe, half queasy to hear my once Earl Grey dad so comfortable with all this terminology. He even said *choon* in the correct street parlance when his current favourite dance track came on Kiss FM, which was as synonymous with his lounge now as Magic FM was with a GP's waiting room.

Ice, Tina, yaba, crank isn't known as one of the most addictive of drugs for nothing. I felt nothing short of orgasmic after one puff of it and I could make that feeling last for hours, so even if not one of those women came back to mine after all those dates, my body was under the impression they had, and all on the same night.

No sleep imminent, I would ride out my high sitting next to Dad at his desk as he worked. To anyone I hadn't met before (and to some I had) Dad would invariably introduce me as his 'son and heir', and deep in those few dark recesses of my brain that had somehow dodged the deluge of psychoactives, a little thought would squeak out, 'What exactly am I inheriting here?'

As the deal was done and intelligent adult conversation flowed, a little sample of Tina would be lit and passed round the desk, of which I would partake, eager not to be the little boy waiting for his dad to take him to Hamleys any longer, but instead a fully-fledged drug baron's heir. It was all so *Godfather*-ish – that is, if Brando's part was played by, say, a shaven-headed Rick Moranis (of *Honey, I Shrunk the Kids* fame) and Pacino, the 'heir', was played by, say, Hugh Jackman… OK, Leonardo DiCaprio… OK, OK, Daniel Radcliffe.

I liked to think I was doing my bit to normalise the experience for the customers too, helping to drag it all out of the gutter: this was a decent man with a decent son, selling quality goods to decent people only; as far from the cliché of a squat strewn with used needles, the walls smeared with the excrement of incontinent, hallucinating junkies as you could imagine.

Meanwhile, I was having a ball working my way through Jdate.com and the latest lady on my list was called Jo. She only had one picture on her profile – usually cause for alarm bells to ring in the ears of any experienced J-dater like myself – but since this one photo was particularly stunning I made an exception. How gracious of me! It did help that I could see she had already favourited me, so I figured I might be on to a winner. And a few well-placed lines of cheeky banter about the 1970s calling up wanting her dress back and some reverse psychology about me not being totally sure about going on a date with someone like her, had her handing over her phone number faster than you can say James Bond and the first date was arranged at her request in the gentrified and very popular pub on Haverstock Hill, imaginatively named The Hill.

The place was packed, as ever, so no dark corners to hide in, but I suppose that was exactly why Jo chose it – in case I turned out to be a slimy octopus of a J-date. Nevertheless we got on famously, chatted endlessly, shared a kiss and booked in a second date. I shouldn't have been surprised, this was my usual form these days, but I still couldn't help walking home after a date like this like a blind man healed, blinking at the wonder of this brave new world.

Things moved quickly with Jo, quicker than with anyone else I'd dated recently. Within a month we'd agreed to go on our first holiday together, to the shock of Will.

'That's a bit sudden, mate. Are you sure you're ready to spend so much time in each other's pockets?'

And Jake. 'Prague? In December? At least take her somewhere hot where she'll always have her kit off on the beach.'

'It's not that sudden. I mean, it's a good way to find out if we can stand each other for long periods. Besides, no one's getting any younger here. Why not get on with it?'

'You're a braver man than I,' Jake sighed and went back to shooting up zombies.

Way before the holiday I was beginning to think Jo might be *The One* so I was really keen for her to meet Dad, but not in the reckless way I had introduced Kate to him. I was not going to sabotage this relationship, so the venue for this meeting was to be a nice restaurant – as opposed to Dad's crack den/sex dungeon of a flat, no matter how decent a crack den/sex dungeon I told myself it was.

I was excited to see how Jo and Dad got on, despite the fact that he was looking more gaunt than ever, acting even more erratically, and throwing Elton John style tantrums whenever we argued, but to be honest I really didn't know how long he had left the way he was going, so I was desperate to get them together as soon as possible.

Dad turning up on time, or at all, was always going to be an issue, so this time, to try to minimise the chance of him cocking up, I booked a table at a restaurant literally around the corner from his flat, less than a five-minute walk. There wasn't another eating establishment closer to his home apart from the grotty and erroneously named Perfect Fried Chicken.

'OK, Dad, we're all booked. Seven thirty, OK? Can't wait for you to meet her.'

'Yeah. Great.' He sounded distracted, as usual. Sounded like he thought it was as *great* as Perfect Fried Chicken's fried chicken was perfect.

'Everything all right?' Jo asked over my shoulder.

'My dad's a little scatty these days.' I spoke like PM Gordon Brown's chief spin doctor: 'I'm afraid he has… experimented with [i.e. is addicted to] a few [any and all] drugs in the past [few minutes, hours, days, weeks, months, years], so bear with him, eh?'

I thought that was plenty to reveal at this point. I didn't want to scare her off.

We arrived at 7.30 p.m. precisely – I still had not learnt to be half an hour late when meeting dad to considerably reduce my own waiting time and stress levels – and at 8 p.m., after we'd both had a couple of glasses of wine, I called Dad.

'Just finishing a few things off, son,' he chirped.

Finishing what? A particularly long line of bugle?

'I'll be with you very soon.'

'When's soon, Dad?' I said pointlessly.

'Soon,' he sang and hung up.

At 9 p.m. he rolled in. And I mean *rolled* in. Though we were two minutes' walk from his home he turned up in a gold Silver Shadow Rolls Royce. Jo nearly spat her Chardonnay across the room as I nearly choked on the crumbs of the breadstick I inhaled. Dad bounded in and sat down, greeting Jo warmly, doing his best to be friendly, though he was clearly jittery.

'So sorry I'm late,' he simpered to Jo, as if he had never been late in his life.

I waited for the excuse. He didn't even bother. He just sat there, his ever-shrinking shoulders hunched, clutching a green khaki bag protectively.

'Nice car,' I said.

'Thanks, son,' was all he said as if I'd just commented on his shirt.

After a bit more small talk, we finally got to order and Jo went to the bathroom.

'What's up, Dad? You seem nervous.'

'Of course I'm nervous, son. I'm worried what she'll think of me. I mean, she's your new girlfriend. And not just any old girlfriend, the way you've been going on about her. She obviously means a lot to you. So I want to make a good impression.'

'Then try turning up less than an hour and a half late,' I wanted to say, but I drowned the words in the white wine. Actually I was surprised by his insecurity. Despite the terrible state he was in, he was self-aware enough to worry about making a good impression on Jo. The old Dad is still in there, I thought, somewhere.

He clutched the green khaki satchel tighter to his chest. That reminded me of the old Dad too, with his Tesco carrier bag with his asthma inhalers, five Kleenex tissues, diary and pen. This bag had replaced the Tesco carrier bag – more cool to be seen with in a club, he'd obviously been told. It still contained the inhalers, the tissues, the diary and the pen, but now it also housed a twenty-pack of Marlboro Lights, a wad of fifty-pound notes, condoms and a crystal meth pipe. No wonder he never loosened his grip on it.

The dinner went pretty smoothly, Dad even pulling out some old jokes which had me smiling, recalling the one about putting the kettle on he used to use with Mum, and even the one about being rolled off the ship during our cruise from New York. Jo reciprocated with her own corny jokes, which seemed to put Dad at ease – here was a lady who got him. Well, not all of him, obviously. Not yet. I couldn't explain to her right then, for example, why he disappeared to the bathroom for over twenty minutes.

'Oh, have some more runner beans, darling, my dad's just gone for a hit of crystal meth.'

Jo and I were so plastered by the time Dad arrived nothing would have fazed us anyway, and in the haze of intoxication, his dysfunctional state seemed to be a lighter, more solvable challenge. It was just in the harsh light of sobriety the next morning that the sadness and sense of impending doom would kick back in again.

When it came to paying the bill, Dad insisted he pay and took his wad of fifty-pound notes out of his trusty bag. Jo's eyes bulged, not without a little thrill, I'm sure, that she was potentially marrying into money here. Little did she know it was the wrong kind of money.

As Dad drove away in his ostentatiously gaudy motor, I put my arm around Jo, and we waved him off like a couple of parents saying goodbye to their child as he set off for his first term at university. I was delighted that Jo and Dad had got on so well, and more convinced than ever that she was going to be my wife. My instinct, however, about the lack of time my Dad had left was about to be proved true – but not in the way I had thought.

CHAPTER 26

CARRY ON ABROAD

I couldn't shake this feeling that time was running out for Dad. I confided in Ruth about it and, instead of telling me to let him perish in a pile of his own vomit, which wouldn't have been an unwarranted request given his behaviour at her partner's funeral, she suggested I ask him to go on a short holiday, just him and me, a chance to spend quality time together.

'Something which if you don't do now you might regret if you don't get the chance again,' Ruth said gently, her words aching with still-recent experience.

'I'd love to, but he's bound to have something "better" to do.'

'You won't know if you don't try,' was Ruth's sagacious response and so I popped the question next time I went round his flat.

'Hey, Dad, how about we have a nice relaxing trip somewhere? Some quality father-son time? Give us a chance to catch up properly. I mean, we can hardly do that here, can we?'

I shrugged as the buzzer went yet again and he jumped up to ask some waif camping out on his sofa to let whoever it was in while he finished measuring out a few grams of meth to the bouncer filling his office, who, if my Dad's and the waif's example was anything to go by, would soon only be able to fill a particularly narrow airplane bathroom door.

'OK, son,' he said.

I didn't think he was high at the time, but frankly I couldn't care less, as long as he was saying yes. I virtually booked the tickets to Minorca on the spot before he could have one of his turns and start accusing me of trying to trick him into leaving his flat, or something equally paranoid.

The flight was from Heathrow, one morning late that summer, and I made sure I turned up at his flat with tonnes of time to spare – after all, I may have been deficient in many areas, but I didn't have learning difficulties.

He had not even begun packing when I arrived – no surprise there. I was totally zen about that and offered to pick out a few tank tops for him – what else!

Then his phone began ringing ceaselessly and even though he answered every call, and even though I started to look at my watch and bite my tongue a little, I knew everything was going to be just fine. Om!

Then visitors began arriving as if he'd advertised a bank holiday summer sale on class A's – *Buy now with nothing to pay until your next score!* – and as I was pushed aside by the stream of shoppers tramping in and out, I have to admit my chi was starting to chafe somewhat, rubbed the wrong way as it was by my FUCKING FATHER!

When we finally got out of that hellhole we were running very late, but Dad insisted upon driving in his Silver Shadow Roller to a specific travel agency to exchange his currency because it offered the 'best deal in London'.

'Really, Dad? I mean, what does a few cents difference make to a bloke who drives a fucking gold Rolls Royce?'

'Look after the pennies and the pounds will take care of themselves, son.'

Of course, the travel agency in question might as well have been in Cornwall, it was so far out of our way. And perhaps equally predictable was, the fact that it was closed when we got there. I was the one who should have been banging my head off the kerb right then, but instead I just let out a little fart of a snipe, something like, 'You did this on purpose, didn't you, trying to make us late.' And Dad went full-on Elton on me, banging the steering wheel repeatedly, stamping his feet and screaming in a manner that would compete with the most petulant toddler – a very foul-mouthed petulant toddler.

'Stop fucking pushing me, I don't even want to go on this fucking stupid holiday!'

After many deep breaths and much counting to ten we found another bureau de change and hit the motorway. In a frightening repetition of our trip back from The Darkness concert in San

Diego five years before, Dad started shifting about in the driving seat, biting his lip, clearly desperately trying to stay awake since it was so unusual for him to be up at this godly hour.

'You OK, Dad?' I grumbled. 'Look, if you're falling asleep, please just let me drive. I don't want to die today.'

'No, no, I'm fine.'

'Really?'

'Yes.'

We both sat in sulky silence for five minutes until his head dropped. Not just slightly lolled, no! That head fell like a big-boned monarchist in the French Revolution. Since we were going at 70 mph at the time my eyes were glued on him because I, unlike him, valued my life, so I grabbed the steering wheel and kept us on course.

'For fuck's sake!'

He snapped back awake.

'For fuck's sake, just let me drive!'

'I'm OK now, that will have woken me up.'

'Oh, I'm so glad that woke you up, Dad, but next time perhaps you could try coffee like everyone else, or even a slap round the face, which I'd gladly help out with by the way, instead of trying to kill us both as your preferred means of stimulant.'

'It won't happen again,' he said with a hint of contrite schoolboy, and a liberal sprinkling of sarcastic parent.

Five minutes later it did happen again, and I wondered if those learning difficulties I'd insisted I didn't possess were actually a seriously undiagnosed problem of mine. I made a mental note to go and see a special needs expert as soon as we got back from Minorca and then filled the car with a torrent of abuse. Why was I even going through with this? Why didn't I stop the car, get out and take the tube home right now? What made me think this holiday was going to be a bundle of laughs, when the overture was such a fucking tragedy?

The motorway on the approach to Heathrow was totally gridlocked.

'OF COURSE IT IS!' I nearly laughed. Nearly. And if I didn't know better I would have sworn every driver in this traffic jam was a friend or client of Dad's who he'd drafted in to make damn sure we missed that flight, the woman at the check-in desk included.

'Sorry, sir, the gate is closed.'

'But can't you make an exception, we could run—'

'Sir, feel free to run…'

'Really?'

'… to Minorca, yes, because the plane has already taken off. So unless you'd like me to ask it to turn around and come and pick up two passengers that couldn't manage their time adequately, I suggest you go over there and try to find another flight.'

I looked at Dad. Was that a smirk that crossed his face? Was he amused at the check-in assistant's oh-so-hilarious wit, or was he enjoying the fact we'd missed the flight? Perhaps it was me who was the paranoid one now, since Dad said in consoling tones, 'Don't worry, as the lady says, there are other flights to Minorca today. Let's go and find one.'

'But we won't get a refund on this flight. That money's gone up in smoke.'

'Well, these things happen.' Dad smiled.

Oh, yes, silly me. Just how much money had gone up in smoke and into his lungs over the past decade? And yet still he had so much more to burn, as the wad of red bank notes in his trusty satchel testified.

'Yes, there is another flight today, sir,' said a far more pleasant and helpful assistant.

'Cool!'

'But it's not until this evening.'

'Oh.'

'And it's flying out of Luton airport.'

Unhelpful, nasty bitch!

We booked the flight and I suggested we head straight for the airport at a leisurely pace. There we could take it easy and while away the hours until the evening flight.

'Let's just stop by Sainsbury's first though, son.'

'Are you serious?'

'Yes, we've got loads of time now. They've got some great deals on at the moment.'

'No, we're going straight to the airport. You can shop in duty free if you want to.'

So there I was in the cereal aisle of an East London Sainsbury's, following my dad about in wide-eyed resignation at the ridiculousness of the situation.

'Oh wow, James, you see, I told you they had good deals on. Sugar Puffs are buy one get one free and they've got a coupon on the back, collect ten coupons for a free box of Ready Brek. What a steal!'

I didn't point out the fact that half of the cupboards in his kitchen were already full to bursting with boxes of Sugar Puffs – they were his current obsession. It wouldn't have stopped him. He was over the moon at saving ninety pence on every box of cereal. Completely irrational given the thousands he was raking in every week dealing, but he actually looked happier than I'd seen him in a long while, so who was I to piss on his puffs?

'I'll just take this lot home,' he smiled, 'then we can head for the airport.'

'No, Dad, no need to go home, they'll keep in the boot of your car for a week.'

And there I was back in his flat watching him carefully stack boxes of Sugar Puffs into spaces that were crying out to be filled with the odd vegetable or piece of fruit. And then he started making calls and pottering about in his office with all the contentment of a cat kneading a sun-drenched cushion. There were, however, other sun-drenched cushions around a pool on an island in the middle of the Mediterranean waiting for me and I wasn't about to miss out on them again.

'Dad, you know all that time we had to get to Luton and hang about until the evening flight?'

'Yes.'

'Well, we don't have it anymore. If we don't leave now, we'll miss that flight too.'

Incredibly he came and incredibly, despite the journey there being a blur of stress and anxiety, we made it through check-in and into security.

'Sir,' said a swarthy, hairy-armed security guard. 'I just need to take a look in your bag.'

I felt like someone had opened a trap door in my feet and my entire blood supply had fallen out. I watched with eyes like saucers – saucers belonging to a particularly genteel fairy-tale giant who goes in for tea parties – as the hairy arms delved into Dad's khaki satchel. I watched them rummage around and waited for them to pull out the crack pipe and a big bag of meth. But Dad wasn't a complete fuck-up. There were no drugs. The hairy arm pulled out a camcorder instead and examined it with faux forensicality.

'Oh thanks!' Dad snapped. 'I was going to surprise my son with that, and now you've ruined it.'

'I'm sorry, sir, but it's standard procedure, we have to check some bags. I didn't mean to upset you.'

'Yes you did! You did it on purpose.'

I was taken aback. Not just because Dad was trying to pick a fight with airport security, but mainly because he'd had the presence of mind and generosity of spirit to think about bringing a gift for me on a holiday that he seemed to be doing everything in his power to screw up. The gesture was one of those rare hints I clung on to in those dark days; glimmers of hope that he could still come through this, that his old self was still in there, waiting to be rescued. But right now the most important thing was to calm him down and hurry him along so that we didn't get chucked out of the airport or miss this flight too.

When we got to the gate it was unsettlingly deserted. But not closed. Everyone was boarded, except us. The ground staff rushed us on, we sat down and I whispered to Dad with a chuckle of relief, 'Bloody hell, Dad, I thought that guard was going to pull a load of meth out of that bag for a minute there.

'Give me some credit, son. I know not to take drugs on an airplane.'

'Thank God,' I sighed and sank into my seat, as far as a six-foot bloke can sink into an EasyJet seat.

'No, the drugs are in my hold luggage,' he said and passed out.

He was joking. I think. No, I'm pretty sure he was joking and that he brought no drugs with him on our little holiday, hence all the procrastination. It filled me with pride that this drug addict had been willing (well, reluctantly willing) to go for five days without drugs in order to spend time with his son. Perhaps he too knew that the time we had was, as they say, borrowed time, but anyway I saw his coming as another chink in his dark armour with the potential to let the light flood through eventually. The only trouble was, with no drugs to keep him up, he spent the five days of our holiday on a massive comedown.

I would knock on his door every morning. 'Dad, I'm going down for breakfast. Coming?'

Nothing.

'Dad?' Knock, knock. 'Dad?'

Groans from inside. 'I'm tired, James. I need more sleep. Catch you by the pool later.'

After breakfast I'd knock again. 'Dad, coming to the pool?'

'I'll catch you up.'

Lunchtime came and still no sign of Dad, so I'd go back to the pool like Billy No-Mates until dinner, when hunger would finally drive Dad to join me. I'd be knocking back the whiskey, he'd be on Diet Coke (of course! God forbid he drank something as terrible as alcohol) and we'd finally get a chance to chat, though the chat, like the holiday, was pretty one-sided.

'Your gums look sore, Dad,' I said as he nibbled on a budgerigar-sized portion of paella.

'Ah yeah, that's from the gum infections I've been getting recently. They last for weeks, you know, and leave me bedridden. I really must get the dentist to do something about it.'

I didn't think it was the dentist who was the one who needed to do something about it. The gum infections were just one of many long, drawn-out illnesses he was succumbing to on a regular basis these days. I wanted to tell him how worried I was but, the paella having been abandoned, he was already slinking off back to bed.

And so this pattern would repeat itself for the entire trip. I might as well have gone on my own. It just wasn't normal for someone to sleep that much. To me it demonstrated just how worn out, how completely exhausted his mind and body were. My anger with him turned to deep concern. Was he really getting so little sleep at home? Is this how much meth can screw your body up? I was glad he was having a few days off it, but when we got back I feared he would go straight back on it.

My deep concern, however, turned back into utter exasperation when on the final day I was helping him pack a bag and the zip broke.

'Bloody hell, James!' he exploded. 'That was your fault for over-packing the thing.'

'Sorry.'

'Do you know how much that bag cost?'

'I said I'm sorry. I'm sure you could afford ten more just like it anyway.'

'That's not the point.'

Not only did he throw his toys out of the pram but he actually threw a bedside lamp across the room at this point.

'Fuck! Don't be so dramatic, Dad.'

'Well, if I'm so dramatic why don't you find your own way home?'

And so we spent the next few hours before we left the hotel on sun loungers by the pool – at last by the pool together! – only we stroppily sat at opposite ends, after which we took separate cabs to the airport and stood in separate lines to check-in – me recording a minor victory in my head as my queue moved faster than Dad's so I ended up getting checked-in first. We sat far apart on the plane and I was quite prepared to get a taxi home from Luton, but some grunts from Dad at Arrivals indicated that I was allowed to get a lift with him if I wanted, and a few grudging grumbles from me were my way of accepting his generous offer.

A week or so later, back in my place in Kings Cross, I picked up a message on my mobile. It was from Dad. He was very apologetic, conceding that he had been in the wrong.

'You always hurt the ones you love the most,' he said.

You do, Dad. *You* do.

CHAPTER 27

SLIDING DOORS

A Monday morning at work – not ever the most uplifting of times. A cold, wet Monday morning in December – that just rubs salt in the wound. But at least I had a new job. And it had ironically come from an email I'd sent while at my last role, the one I was so unceremoniously kicked out of. I'd decided then to follow my new-found passion, the latest marketing discipline which was still in its infancy: social media. I found one of the only specialist social media agencies in London and fired off an email. A conversation had ensued over the summer and that led to an interview. Well, now I'd found Jo, I needed to behave like a responsible adult if I was to hold on to her. Besides, full and uninterrupted coverage of the Ashes was over.

My mobile rings as I sit at my desk. I don't recognise the number, but instead of letting it go to answerphone and expecting a voicemail from some schmuck asking me if I have mistakenly taken out PPI or telling me about the damages I could claim for a car accident I've never had, I answer it, perhaps in the vain hope that it will be some unexpected ray of sunshine to brighten up my day.

'Hello?'

'Hello. Is this James Lubbock?'

'Yes it is.'

'Ah, hi, James. My name's John. I'm a good friend of your dad's.'

Fuck. It's happened at last. He's been found dead. I knew it would come to this. The only question was: drug overdose or killed by an unhinged client?

'Oh yes? How can I help?' I said as if it was just an employee at the detergent firm whose account I was managing.

'Erm, I'm afraid your father's been arrested...'

The rest of the call was a haze of words. A bit like when Ruth had called and told me things had *gone south* with Mum, I both grabbed at all the words I heard and analysed them to death while being buffeted by a whirlwind of possibilities, emotions, implications, next steps, practicalities. Some of the words I processed revealed that John was not only a good friend of my dad's but his solicitor too. I stumbled out of the office, suddenly convinced my mobile had a megaphone attached to it broadcasting my dirty laundry to all my colleagues, and found myself pacing up and down Greek Street, outside a West End theatre. This just added to the surreal effect of the call as I discussed life-changing events amidst a throng of tourists whose biggest concerns then seemed to be if they were going to get tickets to see *Jersey Boys* or not. Other words and phrases I clung on to as they whistled through my head were 'flat was raided', 'Dad was asleep in a chair', 'significant quantities of drugs found', 'large amounts of cash', 'multiple pieces of incriminating of evidence'. I got the picture. There may have been a slight shiver of relief that he was not dead after all, but it was quickly shoved out the way, as I was by the theatregoers, and replaced with concern over the state he was in now. John made no bones about it.

'I've demanded he gets put on suicide watch. I mean, he's hysterical, manic; he's not in a good way at all, James.'

'Well, you wouldn't be, would you, I mean, if you'd just lost everything, and been banged up without so much as your next fix to ease the pain.'

Lost everything. Had he lost everything? Shit! I suppose he had in the sense of the money and the lifestyle and the people he'd been enjoying for the past decade. He'd lost the love of his life to cancer and most of his family didn't speak to him anymore. And now he'd lost his freedom.

'He told me you were about to go on holiday with your girlfriend to Prague.'

'He remembered that?'

'Yes, and he told me to tell you he wanted you to go, don't stay back because of this. And I think he's right. Look, to be honest with you, James, you should look after yourself at a time like this. Your dad's an old man; it's possible he won't see the right side of a prison wall ever again, but you, you've got the rest of your life ahead of you…'

I wasn't really listening to this rather harsh but pragmatic advice from the solicitor; I was still bathing in the knowledge that Dad even paid attention to details like my holiday with Jo. It flooded my torso with a warmth that kept the cold December air at bay for a lot longer than my turtleneck was capable of – yes, this may have been my coming-of-age moment, but there were some fashion faux pas that I was never going to grow out of.

And that's when I knew – with that sensation of warmth rather than the sartorial self-consciousness – he hadn't lost everything. Not everything. He still had me.

I had a thousand questions I wanted to ask, among them: where was he? When could I see him? What about court? I felt pity for the old man John spoke of, anger at having to face this nightmare, which was not of my making, stupid and naive for even being shocked that this phone call was happening: all those tiny glimmers of hope I had turned into solar flares of optimism! What a deluded fool I was! As deluded as he was for thinking he was never going to get caught.

'No, no, I'm not going to be arrested, James. I'm small fry. The police aren't interested in a small-time deal – I mean someone like me. Besides I'm only dea—supplying my friends, just a small group of people that I know and trust.'

But he wasn't small fry anymore. Not with a gold Rolls Royce and fifty grand in cash in a Tupperware box in his filing cabinet.

I could have threatened never to see him again unless he stopped what he was doing – perhaps that would have jolted him out of the dealing and the drug-taking – but I am still sure to this day that if I had gone down that route I would've lost him forever.

John offered to come round to my flat that evening, drop off a copy of the police report and answer any more questions I might have at that point. I think he knew as well as I did that there were just too many questions to deal with on the phone right now, most of them bottlenecking in my throat with all the truculence with which the Four Seasons' fans vied for admittance to the theatre, causing me to become less and less coherent.

I stood there in the street getting tutted at by a million Londoners hurrying about as only Londoners do. What now? Who you gonna call when your mum's no longer on this planet and your dad is in the slammer?

Ruth, of course.

Ruth was every bit as solid as I needed her to be right then. She was sympathetic, but balanced with that was a practical consideration that I had barely thought about since John had first called.

'You need to protect yourself, James. Simply by association with Richard you could be under investigation. It's admirable the way you've not abandoned him, but the regular contact you've had means you could well be a suspect too.' She sighed. The exhalation was full of sadness. 'Do you want me to fly over?'

Ruth had moved back to Vermont after Mum had died and though I knew she was always there for me on the end of the line, I could feel every one of the 3240 miles between us stretching out now to the point of snapping. Her offer brought a sense of loneliness, the first but not the last time that emotion would hit me. I was an only child, I came from a small family and Mum was gone. But stronger than that was the feeling that no one could really help me anyway – this was my problem and I just had to deal with it myself. He was *my* dad, I was the only person he really had at this time and I knew he would be looking to me for help and support regularly as he tried to sort out this mess and minimise the damage.

'No, it's OK, Ruth. Thanks, but I'll be fine.'

'What about Jo?'

'Oh shit!'

Did I say I'd be fine? Jo and I were due to fly to Prague tomorrow. Not surprisingly our holiday had been pushed to the back of my mind a little by recent events; a holiday that, should I even go on it now, was bound to be interrupted at some points by calls from John or even the police. I had to let her know what was going on, but how do you break something like that to the girlfriend you've only known for a few of months without her running for the hills? I had already decided weeks ago that I would tell Jo about Dad's drug addiction and even the dealing, but at a more appropriate time – because there is, of course, an appropriate time to tell someone you're head over heels in love with that your father's a meth head and a drug baron, isn't there? But now my hand had been forced, and like the pilot who landed an Airbus A320 on the Hudson River earlier that year, I just hoped Jo's response would be equally cool and level-headed when the shit-covered birds hit the jet engine.

I got home and stared at the empty suitcase I'd automatically opened on my bed ready to pack. But pack for where? The holiday to Prague of course, you idiot, one half of me said to the other half − the half that had just suggested this suitcase could be packed with everything I needed to do a runner to some anonymous tropical island where I could live out my days free of all this insanity and free from the cops when they came to arrest me, wrongly, for being Dad's narcotics business partner. So instead of packing some budgie-smuggler speedos, some enormous concealing shades and a lifetime's supply of sun lotion, I packed for a cold crisp week in the Czech Republic and then, bizarrely wishing I had a hit of meth to take the edge of this moment, I dialled Jo's number.

'Hey, gorgeous!' Her voice was so carefree it made me want to cry. 'All ready for tomorrow?'

I had no idea what tomorrow would bring anymore so I couldn't really answer in the affirmative. Instead I answered like a politician, 'Are *you*?'

'Well, I thought I was, then I changed my mind about what shoes to take and now I can barely fit it all in. And if I do then I'm worried I'll be over the baggage allowance limit. The

weather forecast says it will be dry, but if it does rain… what
do you think?'

Just tell her! Tell her right now!

I took a deep breath. 'Jo?'

'Mmm?'

'Erm, look… you see, er, there's something I have to tell you,
but it would be better if I didn't do it on the phone. Can you
come over to the flat now?'

The phone went silent for a second. I thought she'd hung
up until I heard her voice, now not so carefree, but trembling
under the weight of some unknown trauma which would most
definitely put her well over the baggage allowance limit.

'What is it, James?'

'Come over!'

'No, you fucking tell me what it is right now! You can't do
that to me, you can't tell me you've got something to tell me then
make me wait until I get to yours, worrying all the way what I'm
about to walk into!'

The sound of Dad's voice from eight years ago came into my
ear like a crossline.

'Let's go for dinner at that lovely French place. Just me and you.'

What would have happened if I hadn't have let him hang up
like that that day in 2002? What would have happened if I had
made him tell me his news over the phone and we had never gone
to La Bonne Heure that night? Would shifting just one thread in
the tapestry of his life have meant that all the future mess could

have been unravelled and another more attractive picture could have assembled itself over the coming years? It was a *Sliding Doors* fantasy, of course, but one that I didn't have time to play then. Jo wasn't going to allow it.

'Jo—'

'No, James, whatever it is, you need to tell me right now.'

'OK, erm. Where do I start?'

'Try the beginning,' she said with a mix of irritation and coaxing.

I took a breath, so deep it made me realise my lungs were bigger than I gave them credit for. 'Well, it all started back in 2002 when my dad revealed to me that he was… gay.' And I related the whole tale to her, just as I have to you, dear reader, warts, gingivitis, the honey monster and all. I heard nothing from Jo during the entire story, except for a few sniffs and ah-huh's, encouraging me to go on. When I finally got to the end – well, not the *end*-end, as you can see there are quite few pages left to go – but when I got to the part about Dad being arrested I stopped speaking and waited for the onslaught from my soon to be ex-girlfriend.

'Oh my gosh!' she laughed. She laughed? Yes, she laughed! She laughed the laugh of the recently reprieved death-rower (that's an inmate of Death Row as opposed to a suicidal white water rafter). 'Oh my gosh,' she said. 'I thought you were going to dump me.'

CHAPTER 28
CAUGHT BY THE FUZZ

After Jo had finished hyperventilating with relief, she quickly became concerned for me and instantly supportive. She insisted that I come over and spend the night with her before we left for the airport in the morning. Not only was the holiday still on, the relationship was too, which was so much more than I had bargained for after that phone call. I couldn't wait to get over to her place, but before I left John arrived as promised.

John was a reassuringly suave solicitor with the cologne and fresh breath to match. He read out the police report to me and I hung on every minty word, not unlike Jo had just done as I'd related the story of the past decade or so of my life, except she couldn't smell my breath down the phone of course, which was just as well because I'd recently gorged on some particularly unkosher comfort food to ease the shock of all this madness. John reiterated the seriousness of the situation – if ever there was an example of a drug dealer being caught red-handed, this was it: wads of cash in boxes, significant quantities of different drugs, most of them class A, drug paraphernalia and lots of corroborating evidence to wrap up the prosecution's case nicely. Disturbingly (in addition to all the firm evidence) the police seemed to be suggesting that Dad was using the adjacent flat, which he also owned, as some sort of escape route. Completely ridiculous, of course – it was just a storeroom for his hoards of junk – but this was the first insight I had that sometimes the boys in blue will use even the flimsiest of evidence to bolster their case and push for the longest sentence possible.

John read on, 'The suspect was found asleep in an armchair wearing just a tank top, no trousers or underwear.'

Oh my God! Until that point I had forgotten about all the other things the cops would have found as they raided the flat – the second bedroom with its S&M swing and paraphernalia of a sexual kind. Trying to wipe from my mind the image of Dad being caught by the fuzz (depending on where the cops grabbed him of course) and wipe the smirk from my face as the indignity of his situation tickled me in a way that it shouldn't, I asked John what happened now.

'You need to arrange a visit.'

Barely had I shut the door behind John when the phone rang.

'Son?'

'Dad?'

'James. It's good to hear your voice. Now, first thing's first: do you have a pen? You need to write this number down: BN8786. That's my prisoner number.'

I wrote it down but it was soon seared onto my brain, where it remained for many years like a scar.

'Dad?' I had to ask again because the tone of this dad's voice was not the mangled, hysterical, hare-brained tone I'd expected to hear, especially after what John had said about his condition. This dad was surprisingly like the old dad and it was as much of a shock to me as Rage Against the Machine being Christmas number one that month was to the little X-Factor puppet they'd kept off the top spot.

Dad was clear-headed, rational, his good head for numbers evidently returned – he had already memorised his prison number and had even remembered my mobile number off by heart (I mean, who knows anyone's mobile number off by heart in this age of imported contact lists and one-touch dial?). These were the positive parts of Dad's autistic obsessiveness, which had me following him round Sainsbury's while he added to his stockpile of Sugar Puffs like some hypoglycaemic squirrel.

'I begged the warden for five minutes to call you. He was very accommodating.'

I prayed that that meant it was a humane and merciful environment he was stuck in and not one where favours were given in return for the kind of actions blokes dressed in leather chaps usually meted out in Dad's spare room.

'Are you OK?' I said, wincing at the sheer inadequacy of such a question.

'Yes, yes, not bad considering. Now, you're off to Prague tomorrow with Jo, is that right?'

'Well, that was the plan, but not—'

'No, no, you must go. No point in staying here because of me. It will take a few weeks for a visit to get arranged anyway so there's absolutely nothing you can do until then. I want you to go. Have a break. My God, you deserve it.'

'Are you sure?'

'Yes, yes.'

It was a comfort to hear him say this with such certainty. It made me feel better about going – and I wanted so badly to get away, especially with Jo.

'James?'

'Yeah?'

'I am so sorry. For everything. And I love you.'

He hadn't said that to me in years. Pulling those three words out of himself seemed to unblock something in him then and his tears came pouring down the line. He was a gibbering mess, but at least now he was a mess that I recognised.

CHAPTER 29
SLEUTH

The lift was out of service, as it had once been when I'd staggered up the stairwell hungover, passing Diane, Dad's secretary, on her way down and out of Dad's life. So I staggered all the way up to the seventeenth floor again today, not reeling from a hangover this time, but from the weight of the new and very sober responsibility on my shoulders. When I got to Dad's flat the solid mahogany door that had always graced the entrance to the luxury apartment was now smashed to bits, and sheets of corrugated iron stuck across it like some hastily applied, and no doubt very uncomfortable, band aids.

Detective Inspector Tyson, in charge of Dad's case, met me at the doorway and guided me through the obstacle course of sheet metal, into the flat that was once a hive of activity – illegal activity mostly – and buzzing with visitors – most of them buzzing themselves on psychoactive narcotics. It was downright weird to get nostalgic about the very thing I wanted Dad to stop doing, but now, in this musty, abandoned *Marie Celeste* of an apartment, I could see what a social hub and blissed-out bolthole this had been before.

'Come on in,' said the DI, as if this was his home, which immediately riled me. This was my dad's home, paid for with the hard-earned wages of his numismatic days. And although it looked a bit shabby when he lived here, now it looked like it had been burgled, ironically, since the police had turned over and turned out everything in a bid to unearth more incriminating evidence. 'You're welcome to take whatever you want now. We already have everything we need.' His tone was cordial, frank, he seemed like a straight-up kind of bloke, but I was on my guard. This could be just the good-cop act designed to make me give something away. I didn't need to get into a conversation with this cuckoo in Dad's debauched little nest anyway. My mission (yes, I couldn't help feeling this was all a bit James Bond, even at a time like this) was to try and retrieve any relevant documentation that would help Dad prove that not every penny he had he owed to the state, since after all the criminal proceedings were dealt with there would be the confiscation proceedings, whereby the CPS would put forward a figure they said Dad owed the state based on the amount of money he had supposedly made from drug dealing over the years. The figure was liable to be a hefty one and they were likely to claim most of his properties and assets to pay off the debt. However, everything Dad owned was a result of the legitimate coin dealing he had done for thirty years before he'd even so much as smoked a joint. He stood to lose everything if we couldn't prove that, and I couldn't let that happen. So I gathered what I could from the mess of files and heaps of papers, which would have been in a much more organised state, despite the police intrusion, had Diane never left. I looked around the office at where Di once sat, serenely sensible, prepossessingly proper. There was a serenity about the flat again, now all the actors, musicians, artists and businessmen had fled the haven where they used to score, or catch up with their mates, or roger their lovers, but the serenity was tinged with a sadness now – the flat was having a hangover, a comedown all of its own. Just as a pang of anger towards Dad shot through me for putting me through this shit and, if I'm honest, jeopardising my own inheritance, I unearthed some old Arsenal match programmes, photos of Mum, Dad and me in happier times, letters from Susan and the family in L.A., and the sadness returned with the pervading rush of a meth hit in reverse.

The DI hung around looking quite pleased with himself, since catching Dad was a major coup for him and the Met. As the national newspaper headlines trumpeted:

Detectives seize 'Britain's largest ever haul of crystal meth' worth £1.5 million after raid on suspected dealer's flat.

As I stood among the ruins of Dad's life looking about me for anything else that might save him, the DI said with a wry chuckle, 'I was surprised you weren't arrested when we took in your old man.'

I went white – as white as a bag of particularly pure and incriminating meth – so I turned my face away from him pretending to be focused on more files and invoices. Holy shit, I thought, imagine if they had arrested me! I'm not sure Jo would have seen things in the same cool way as she had done then. And who would have been there to help Dad if I was stuck in jail too?

'Me? Really? Why?' I said with all the cracked falsetto of a teenage choirboy caught with the lead soprano under his cassock. I really didn't have anything to hide, but with Ruth's warning ringing in my ears, I knew I had to be careful not to say anything stupid or something that might pique the curiosity of this East End sleuth.

'Well, you appear in his diary frequently, he notes you coming to visit regularly, which implies you at the very least knew what was going on.'

Oh my God, he's going to arrest me for conspiring to pervert the course of justice or something, I thought.

He must have read my expression – which was then one of an incontinent man in a kilt – because he went on, 'Oh, it's all done and dusted now so don't worry, but I'm just having an open conversation with you. At the time, that evidence could have caused you a bit of grief, you know.'

I was flushed with a sudden sense of gratitude towards this DI, which was no doubt what the smug dick wanted me to feel, but that also brought with it the pang of anger again. And since we were being open and frank I found myself saying, after careful consideration, 'Well, that actually makes me really angry. It's bad enough that he put me through all of this, but to then put me in that position as well, that's just unforgivable.'

It was the truth, but it was also the kind of deflection Freddie Ljungberg would be proud of. It was designed to keep the spotlight off me and try to get a few more nuggets out of the DI, since revelations of the kind he had just made were like a drug I'd been gagging for since that first call from Dad's solicitor. All the questions I had could never be answered, not fully, even by John, and now here was the lead inspector on the case offering transparency (whatever his calculating reasons).

He fiddled with his mobile instead of disclosing any more of the information I thirsted for and so I added, 'And what could I have done anyway? I was in an impossible situation.'

The detective wasn't giving any more away, but he gave me a conciliatory, almost sympathetic look. I was itching to know more – what was it about this flat that made the occupants crave stuff?! – but I thought I should get out while I was still free to do so.

For a few days after that conversation, I was as jumpy as every MP in the country as the expenses scandal raged on, but the call I feared never came and I, like the MPs, breathed a sigh of relief – although I, unlike the MPs, hadn't done a bloody thing wrong in the first place.

CHAPTER 30

THE KEYS TO MY LIFE

April 2010. Just four months but countless phone calls – with Dad, his solicitors, his accountants and the police – later, it was time for Dad to be sentenced. After all the legal wrangling, uncertainty, stress, arguments and general frustration, we were to learn of Dad's fate – he would be going down, no doubt, but for how long?

Caught with 'Britain's largest ever haul of crystal meth', Dad was sure to get a judicial spanking. There were of course many other dealers out there, no doubt trading in far bigger quantities than Dad had been – but he was the knob who got himself caught. They were discreet, he was reckless, they were in control, he was out of it. He 'almost invited the police to catch him' – this was the Met's analysis of the situation and perhaps, like me with Kate, he was subconsciously sabotaging himself, in order to affect the change that he wasn't capable of making any other way. Well, one can dream. Just as I dreamt of how he might be cut some slack by the judge due to his extenuating circumstances: i.e. he had never offended or broken the law once in his life previously, he had been a philanthropist to a certain extent, giving a fair amount of his earnings (long before he became a drug dealer) to charity, and then there was me – apparently we could try and make the case that I had already lost Mum and I needed his support as the only surviving parent, despite the fact that, in the eyes of society, if not in my own, I was a fully grown, independent adult. I was even asked to pen a statement for the judge's review. So I wrote this before the sentencing:

Richard Lubbock is my father – we've always had an extremely close relationship, which became even stronger after the death of my mother, his wife. He's always been there for me and I've got him to thank (as well as my mother) for a very happy childhood and a secure, safe family upbringing. We regularly met up for dinner and watched football together and we both enjoyed each other's company immensely.

I was shocked to discover that my father had been dealing drugs. I was however well aware that the death of my mother had had a deeply profound and negative effect on him as a person and had pushed him into a depression from which it seemed he would never recover. Although I would never condone such behaviour, I believe that he committed these offences as a way to punish himself for what had happened, even though it wasn't his fault. He couldn't come to terms with the loss he had suffered and the drug dealing was perhaps an outlet for his despair and frustration. I do know that despite his naivety, he never meant anyone any harm and is an incredibly gentle soul.

Since my father has been taken into custody, I've tried to get on with my own life the best I can, although it would be untrue to say that it hasn't affected me. Although my friends have been supportive, I've found it difficult to focus at work – I'm a Senior Account Manager at an advertising agency that demands a great deal of effort, work and due diligence – and it has also put a strain on the relationship with my partner, which is a great worry for me.

Although I've seen him as often as I can, this is restricted to weekend visits as I'm unable to take any more time off work during the weekdays. I already miss him hugely and as I don't really have any other close family it has created a significant hole in my life with which, at times, I'm struggling to cope. I understand that whatever happens he'll have a lengthy sentence, but the longer it continues the more it will feel like another major loss in my life as the visits will be nowhere near sufficient for me. I think towards major future events in my life such as my wedding and kids and it makes me incredibly sad to think he won't be around to witness these.

Although I'm his son and therefore biased, I'd urge anyone reading this to consider how he acted as a human being before the tragic death of his wife. He was a loving, supportive father to me, was respected in the coin business as one of the most honest, trustworthy businessmen in the industry, and regularly gave significant amounts to charities he supported. He treated his close friends like family and they responded in kind with love and affection. He's an honourable man who has unfortunately lost perspective in his life and made wrong decisions in the past few years. I'm of course upset with the way he's behaved, but feel desperately sad for him and would urge these factors to be taken into account when sentencing occurs.

Yes, I hammed it up a bit, but in essence it was all true, or at least that's definitely how I felt at the time. I doubt whether it made the slightest bit of difference, but at least I'd tried. I remember feeling quite proud of it, how it was written (perhaps I could get into this writing lark, pen a book one day…), and I hoped it would at least be taken into consideration.

So the big day arrived, and I approached it with a mixture of anticipation and foreboding. I was curious as to how it would pan out, what the atmosphere would be and who would be there – there were a hundred questions running through my mind again, not least: what the fuck was Dad going to say? You see, he'd taken the unorthodox step of insisting that he be allowed to make a personal statement to the court. It had been made clear to him that it was rare for this to happen and would have a negligible impact on what the judge decided, but he wanted to do it anyway. In a sense, the whole case was unorthodox – a previously law-abiding, upstanding, middle-class husband and father, having run a successful business with an office on Regent Street, squandering everything by ditching his current career and selling drugs, with no need for the money or (I believed) life that came with it. So it was fitting, in a way, that the irregularities such as Dad's statement continued.

Dad had also requested that Jo, whom I was now more serious about than ever and whom I had grown so much closer to since revealing Dad's story to her, did not attend the hearing. He was embarrassed, understandably ashamed, to be seen by her in this light, and so she graciously sat outside during it.

I, however, was called in along with the rest of the surprisingly large crowd (who the fuck were all these people?) and took my place in one of the seats at the side. Dad then appeared behind a glass screen as if he was some deceptively benign-looking man-eating shark in an aquarium, gave me a warm but awkward nod and took his seat. Finally, the judge came into the room with his various administrators and we were ready to begin.

This was not the first time I'd visited Isleworth Crown Court since Dad was arrested. There had been a number of previous hearings, to decide things like the date of this final sentencing, the type of sentencing and, right at the start, whether he wanted to plead guilty or not guilty to the initial charges. He pleaded guilty, on the advice that (a) it would lessen his sentence and (b) there wasn't exactly much wiggle room for pleading any other way since he'd been caught, quite literally, with his pants down. But this particular hearing did feel very different from the previous ones. The tension in the room was heightened mainly by the presence of so many more people attending than usual; these people, I soon realised, as they scribbled away and tapped into phones, were journalists, and I felt their eyes on me as much as on Dad. They knew I was his son, and there's nothing like a bit of family drama to add to a good drug bust story, is there? Not that I was going to give them, the real sharks in the room, anything.

The CPS made their case for the gravity and seriousness of the crime, our barrister countered with all the mitigating factors we could come up with, including me, which sent the first lump of the day lodging itself into my throat. But the thing that was going to leave me positively needing the Heimlich manoeuvre was Dad's speech.

He was called up, stewarded to a podium next to the judge and I was acutely aware then that everyone in the room was suddenly far more attentive, focused on this bizarrely meek-looking drugs 'baron' as he shuffled onto the platform. He carried with him some characteristically tatty pieces of paper on which he'd written his speech. I remember willing him on like a father wills their child to remember their lines and sing out loudly at the primary school concert, except here the judgements weren't being made by competitive parents who'd sat up long into the previous night gluing legs onto an octopus costume or painting cereal boxes the colour of a robot. No, the judgement made here today, whatever Freud might say about the primary school concert, would have a far more crucial and far-reaching effect on my dad and all of us who were close to him.

Dad took a deep breath and I instinctively looked around for his khaki bag so I could delve in and offer him a go on his asthma inhaler, but it was nowhere to be seen. He was on his own now. The room took a deep breath too. And Dad began.

The speech was rambling, broken with painfully long pauses as Dad shuffled through his pieces of paper to try and regain his thread, and I cringed. There were a few moments though that had us all on the edge of our seats for the right reasons. He spoke sadly about his own belief that he mainly fell deeper into dealing in response to the death of Mum, with which he had never been able to come to terms, how he had always struggled to come to terms with death, having been poorly treated by his own parents after his much-loved grandmother died when he was a boy – in his eyes they never let him grieve properly and this traumatic event had affected him ever since. He said he'd effectively been punishing himself and those around him as a way of dealing with losing what he once again called his rock and that he didn't need the money – if anything it was more for company, companionship even.

I was about to start cringing again at all this pseudo-psychology when he pleaded, 'Give me back the keys to my life!' It was an emotive statement. All the metaphorical doors he'd closed to himself flashed through my mind – his business, his relationships, his health – and the actual ones: to his flat, which now hung off its hinges with achingly perfect symbolism, and the ones beyond that glass screen with bars and locks to which he most certainly wouldn't have the keys. He recognised he'd made a terrible mistake and begged for a second chance. He mentioned the regret he had for the impact all this had had on me, said he would never be able to forgive himself for leaving me on my own in this way. At that point his voice broke. He paused, gathered himself, and continued. As much as I wanted to bawl my eyes out I focused on maintaining a neutral expression – I didn't want to give the hacks from the press the satisfaction of seeing any more emotion from our family; there had already been enough intrusion.

And the next thing I knew he had finished. I was relieved that it was over and relieved, despite the toe-curling moments, that he had been, I felt, quite successful in conveying his regret, his essential decency and his dissimilarity to the usual suspects in this position. But mostly, I was relieved it was over so the judge could put us out of our misery and tell us the fucking verdict!

The judge looked at his notes, looked up at Dad, looked back down at his notes, held his cleft chin in a pose of deep consideration – and then gave the sentence he'd probably already planned to give hours before.

'You ask for the keys back to your life,' he growled, 'and I can see how much you regret your actions with regards to the hurt and suffering you've caused your son and other loved ones close to you. But your actions have caused a rash of criminality in terms of all the drugs you sold amongst the local community, and you didn't once mention the regret you have for this specific and significant result of your actions. Moreover, while I accept you had a number of reasons for getting involved in this criminal activity, I think the money, in part, *did* attract you. You saw an opportunity and, being the businessman you are, you swooped on it. So, you ask for the keys back to your life. And I will give them back to you…'

What? He's going to let him go?

'…in this way: I sentence you to eight years…'

Dad's legs buckled, as would mine have had I been standing, despite my sense that what the judge had said was fair. I think he was right when he said that Dad didn't (and should have) expressed regret for that 'rash of criminality'. It was an ill-advised omission and I think Dad left it out because he really didn't see it that way. As he'd told me before, if he didn't do it, then someone else would have, and that attitude, of course, would have gone down with the judge like a female Doctor Who would with most of the nerds I knew.

I felt flat, not distressed, because it was what we expected: this was the average precedent for the sort of crime and level of activity in which Dad was involved. There was no mistaking, however, even though Dad would almost certainly serve half the sentence because of his guilty plea, that even four years was a long time, especially for someone of his age. He was sixty-six at the time.

And so to confiscation proceedings. This was to prove, in some ways, even more traumatic and depressing, as the law was heavily weighted towards the state. It was a huge uphill struggle and one that, despite my 007(ish) efforts at his flat that day with DI Tyson, we would ultimately lose.

On the plus side, Dad's health was already improving dramatically since his forced cold turkey in prison. I just hoped it would continue to improve and that the four years, for both of us, would go quickly.

It was of course all over the papers the next day:

Tower Hamlets crystal meth dealer jailed for eight years

Richard Lubbock, 66, was sentenced to eight years in prison on Friday at Isleworth Crown Court, having been found guilty of five counts of possession with intent to supply.

Lubbock was caught last December when police searched a penthouse flat in Commercial Road and discovered the drugs, which included £127,000-worth of Class A substance methamphetamine, also known as crystal meth.

They also discovered £25,640-worth of cocaine, nearly £64,000-worth of amphetamine, alongside significant amounts of ketamine, fluoroamphetamine and 'skunk' cannabis.

According to a police statement, officers found the drugs 'scattered around' the property, with some stored in filing cabinets and inside the kitchen freezer.

Alongside this article was a Met photo of a drawer in Dad's freezer stuffed with bags full of drugs next to his favourite ice cream. I had to laugh. Whereas your average drug dealer might have a Magnum .44 handgun stashed among his gear, Dad had a four-pack of chocolate Magnum bars. It was a picture that perfectly encapsulated the dichotomy of Dad's childish naivety and wanton depravity.

After the hearing I tumbled out of the court into Jo's loving arms. She, of course, never got to see him in the dock and so the one and only time she had met him – when he had pulled up to the restaurant in Limehouse in his gold Rolls Royce – was the last time she would, at least for a couple of years, the Roller now traded in for a Met police sweat-box.

'April is the cruellest month,' as TS Eliot once wrote. And I couldn't agree more. It was the month my mum died and the month (the following year) my dad was sent down, so as the

Jewish faith dictates, just days after Dad was banged up in HMP Brixton, I was standing once again by Mum's grave for the stone-setting ceremony. The bright side, if there was one? Dad could not make me excruciatingly late to this one. He was behind bars and so all appointments, dates and engagements were safe to walk the streets in unharried promptness. And that one little plus sticking up from the negatives like a crucifix just rammed it home how alone I was now in terms of my nuclear family. Yet, as I felt Jo squeeze my arm and looked up to see Susan's face smiling gently at me, I knew I was not really alone. The stone-setting was almost as well attended as Mum's funeral, with the welcome addition of my girlfriend and my second cousin this time.

I felt my phone vibrate in my coat and answered it as planned. It was Dad. I resisted a sarky comment about unusual punctuality, since it would just rub it in how Dad's time was not his to do as he pleased with anymore, and handed the phone over to Susan. It was the first time they'd spoken in years and I watched with pride as Susan's face registered the cousin she had known and loved so long ago, whom she'd thought she had lost forever. I could see her relief to hear Dad sounding more like his normal self; her face reflected my own feelings the first time he called me from prison. She had her Richard back, even if there were steel bars and many miles between them, for now.

CHAPTER 31

APOSTASY
or MOONING GRANDMA

Jo's parents wanted to meet me.

'Shit, Jo, what have you told them?' I said in a hissing whisper as we sat in front of the TV one night as if her parents were in my kitchen, which they weren't, but I continued to speak as if the flat was bugged since, perhaps not surprisingly, I was particularly paranoid these days.

'Nothing. Not about *that* anyway. But we've been going out for months, James, it's not unreasonable for them to want to meet you, is it?'

Unreasonable? As Jewish parents go, it was downright super cool of them to have not interrogated me sooner. Though my world had been put on hold for most of last year as I became intimate with the judicial and penal systems, this request of theirs brought it home to me that life had been going on around me as usual, at its usual pace. Luckily Jo and I had been getting closer and closer so that I didn't embarrass myself in front of her anymore – I mean, I was still a total knob on a regular basis but I had done it so often it was past embarrassing and fast becoming normal – like farting in bed, although, as my painful and noisy bowels would attest every morning in the safety of a locked bathroom, I was yet to reach *that* stage with her. But things were going great and had been for some time. So no, it wasn't unreasonable for her parents to want to meet me, and therefore a lunch in a kosher restaurant was arranged for the following Sunday.

'Does it have to be a kosher restaurant?' I moaned.

'Is the Pope Catholic?' Jo said, confusing me slightly.

'They're so expensive and the menus are so limited.'

'I'm well aware of that,' Jo said. 'But my parents are very traditional that way.'

Luckily, Jo wasn't so much, and no doubt on the morning after the meeting with her parents she'd be watching me tuck into a big juicy bacon sandwich as a remedy for my inevitable hangover.

I was understandably jittery when Sunday came and we arrived, edgily, in Edgware. I wanted to make a good impression. My feelings about Jo were such that I hoped these people would be my in-laws soon enough, so as I followed her in I tried to strike the right balance of confident without being an arse and humble without being… well, an arse. I suppose you could say, in short, I just didn't want to come across as an arse, but when I saw that not only were Jo's parents there, but also her sister and her husband, their two kids and Jo's grandmother, I nearly lost all the composure I'd been working so hard on and became that arse I so feared I would be. And what's more, I couldn't fall back on all those wonderful lines and techniques I'd learnt from the dating gurus unless I wanted to sidle up to Jo's mum and say, 'Damn, if being sexy was a crime, you'd be guilty as charged!' Or whisper into her granny's ear, 'Did you sit in a pile of sugar? Cause you have a pretty sweet ass.'

The other thing I had been worried about as Jo and I got dressed that evening and I got a good look at us both in the mirror, which once again reminded me that I was not only punching well above my weight but was legging it out of the ring having stolen the WBA belt from the rightful champion, was that Jo must have got those good looks of hers from her father and mother, so they were probably both, respectively, intimidatingly suave and stunning creatures. However, that wasn't quite the case.

'Thank God,' I said, shaking Jo's father's hand as my nervousness made my mouth resemble my bowels in said bathroom after a hard night holding it all in next to Jo. 'I feel so much better having actually met you, you know, 'cause I was so worried you'd look like film stars or something, but luckily you don't, you just, er, look, erm…'

'Yes?' Paul said, his grip on my hand getting a little tighter, threateningly tight perhaps.

'Oh, I mean, you just look very… normal.'

'What are we going to drink?' Jo cut in tactfully and her father released my hand, since I'd paid him the biggest compliment any middle-class conservative Jew could wish for: to be normal.

As we ordered drinks, my mouthful of Trebor Extra Strong Mints hopefully masking the skinful of Dutch courage I'd had before we arrived, I fired small talk questions at Jo's parents, trying desperately to keep them from having the time to ask me anything, like, oh I dunno, for example, 'What does your father do?' As they spoke I examined that normalness of theirs a bit more: Jo's dad had a genial face, grey hair, balding, and a smart shirt buttoned over his middle-age spread; Jo's mum had dark-brown, well-kempt hair and she was conservatively yet fashionably dressed. Yes, they bore a startling resemblance, in fact, to my own parents a decade or so ago. They say to nervous performers or public speakers it helps to imagine your audience naked. I often thought that would be a bit of a distraction from remembering your dialogue or your speech, what with all that genitalia lined up in rows in front of you. Anyway, I had a much better technique for getting me through this meeting: I just had to imagine this very normal and respectable pair of heteros donning leather hot pants and dealing class A drugs to the customers while pogoing around the restaurant to Gloria Gaynor off their tits on meth. For me it wasn't a stretch. I mean, if my dad could do it, why couldn't they? So Jo's parents' appearance was not only reassuringly familiar, but it also sent a pang of yearning for the past shooting through me as I realised more than ever I was not a kid anymore.

'You found it OK then?' Jo's mum said.

What, a kosher restaurant in Edgware? How could I miss it? Just follow the Volvos and the black skull caps. 'Oh yes, it's no problem these days with satnavs,' I simpered.

'You live in Kings Cross, don't you?' Jo's dad asked.

I know, it's tantamount to apostasy, me a Jew and not living in North West London! 'I do, yes. I have a flat there.' I thought that was enough detail for now. They didn't need to know my dad owned it. Not that that would have been an anomaly in our community, but it would have brought my dad into the conversation and then it was only a matter of time before they started probing me about him.

'This matzah is bad,' Jo's grandmother piped up, spitting out some of the bread she'd been grazing on.

'It's not matzah, Grandma,' Jo explained. 'It's pitta. It's Italian bread.'

'I thought this was a kosher restaurant,' Grandma grimaced.

'It is.'

'You said it was Italian.'

'I said the bread was Italian.'

'What do the Italians know about kosher?'

'Some of the food is in the Italian style, Grandma, that's all. This place is Jewish,' Jo said, turning the menu over so her grandmother could see the Middle Eastern section, which seemed to reassure her no end.

'So what do you do?' Jo's dad continued.

'I work in advertising,' I said.

'You run your own agency?' he said eagerly.

'No, but I'm an account director.'

'Oh.' Paul took a long sip on his Diet Coke. 'Well… Rob here,' he said, gesturing proudly at his son-in-law. 'He runs his own company. And he's doing very well.'

Of course he does, I thought. Every bloody Jew on the planet seems to run their own company except me. 'Oh, cool. What do you do?' I asked Rob, who was looking enviably cool and sure of himself.

'I'm in marble, mainly. I supply various types of stonework for bathrooms, kitchens, etc. I did one of the Arsenal players' bathrooms once.'

'Oh, Gooner are you?' I said hopefully.

'Spurs actually,' he replied with the kind of confidence that had me suspecting everyone in the restaurant was a Tottenham fan, except me.

But as the meal wore on I realised Rob's attitude wasn't fuelled by the pride his father-in-law had in him, or even by a lunching contingent of the Blue Army; it was the complacency of one who had sat where I was sitting not that long ago and who wasn't the new boy in the family any longer, thanks to my new, bumbling presence. At least I could say I had a job, I reassured myself. If this meeting had taken place less than a year earlier the only thing I could have told Paul was that I was a full-time viewer of the Ashes on telly and a regular visitor at a sordid den of iniquity owned by my dad. As I watched Rob's two perfect kids behaving perfectly, my man-womb told me I wanted kids too. And I wanted to be as great a parent as my mum was to me – apart from her tendency to dress me up like Pee-wee Herman, of course. And I reassured myself again that my parenting might not be as perfect as Rob's, but I would not be dropping any bombshells on my kids… Well, not any with the same explosive content as my dad's, anyway.

Jo's sister hadn't said much so far and as I stole a glance or two in her direction I saw her looking at me with a knowing smile on her face. It was a warm look of sympathy, but I was curious about what this knowing smile indicated she knew. So when I'd carefully choreographed my visit to the toilet to coincide with Jo's return from it I collared her behind a large potted plant and hissed, 'Does your sister know?'

'Well… I had to tell someone, James. You can't keep news like that to yourself.'

'Well *you* can't, that's for sure.'

'James!'

'I'm sorry. It's just that she might blab to someone else.'

'She won't. I know my sister.'

'OK. Sorry.'

'But you know it's only a matter of time before we have to tell my parents, don't you?'

'Yes, yes, but not now, not on the first meeting.'

'OK. But soon. OK?'

'OK.'

We went back to the table and finished the meal without a hitch. In fact, regardless of the fact that I couldn't eat a thing because my stomach was in knots, I was quite enjoying the company of Jo's family and I was quickly coming to the conclusion that I would be very happy to be a part of it – if they'd have me. As we all put on our coats and shuffled towards the exit I made some comment to Jo loudly so that everyone could hear.

'Hopefully I've impressed the future in-laws.' I chuckled theatrically waiting for all the seals of approval to be stamped on my back by the friendly hands of Jo's relatives.

'Well, it's about time Jo settled down,' said her mum. 'And beggars can't be choosers.'

Eh?

'Yes,' said her dad with a mischievous look. 'You're no spring chicken anymore, Jo. It's not like you can afford to be choosy at this stage.'

'Dad!' Jo said.

'Is this one Jewish?' Grandma piped up.

'Yes he is,' Jo's mum said and Grandma seemed appeased.

I didn't know whether to be mortally offended or deliriously happy that Jo's age and me simply being a Jew meant that unless I jumped on the table now and pulled down my trousers, mooning Grandma while chomping on a pulled pork sandwich, I was pretty much welcome in this family. I just hoped that would still be the case when they found out about my dear old dad.

CHAPTER 32
MILK AND MEAT

Until Jo and I got engaged I was more than happy that my knowledge of the local synagogue only extended to its white exterior, which had all the charm of a mausoleum. Now, however, as I entered it for the first time alongside my future father-in-law Paul, I could admire the interior. There was a lot of wood. White wooden ceilings, mahogany adornments and pews that were filling fast with chattering Jews – the men sitting separately from the women, of course, in this United (aka orthodox, aka strictly conservative) shul, as we practising Jews like to call a synagogue. Don't worry, I haven't gone completely bonkers and lost my heretofore steadfast atheism. In fact, if you scratched the surface here you would find most of these regulars did not believe in a supernatural Old Testament God, but rather they were here for a good gossip and a catch up. It was a glorified social club to many and the chatter continued way into the service itself, which had the rabbi shushing the congregation periodically like a school teacher in front of a rowdy class of kids.

The rabbi was not your classic-looking rabbi, i.e. a *Fiddler on the Roof* cast member. He was young... well, my age I'd guess, late thirties, which was pretty young for a rabbi, I thought – or was I getting to that age where everyone in positions of authority, like headteachers and doctors, suddenly seemed to be looking younger, when in fact it was just me who was getting older, ramming it home that by now I should be in one of those positions of authority myself, or at least running my own bloody business like my oh-so-settled brother-in-law? The rabbi was tall and slim, which definitely bucked the trend a little where rabbis were concerned, but he did have the obligatory beard, though his was trimmed and tidy. He spoke quickly, with passion, but always had a twinkle in his eye, as if something was amusing him, a joke was eternally lurking around the corner, and consequently his sermons didn't send me to sleep, which was a first. Dad used to take me to two services a year – the 'big ones': Rosh Hashanah (Jewish New Year, which is like everyone else's New Year, but without the fun) and Yom Kippur – I'd be asleep before the Torah was opened. I liked the fact that this young rabbi didn't appear to take himself too seriously and so I felt he was never likely to force his beliefs on you – or at least that's what I told my heretical self.

As an engaged couple, Jo and I together had to have a meeting at the shul with the rabbi first, then in the run up to the wedding, as the United tradition would have it, I alone would have a few meetings with him at his home. I was more curious than anything to have these meetings and find out more about my culture, although I was also terrified of making any faux pas in the presence of this orthodox man and his family, so as I walked up to his front door I kept telling myself, 'Don't shake her hand, don't shake her hand!' Because in the orthodox tradition, one never touches another man's wife.

As the rabbi's wife greeted me on the doorstep, I stuck out my hand. *Idiot!* Then swept my hand over my head and smoothed down my hair – styling it out, as the kids say these days – my faux pas, that is, not my hair.

Having narrowly averted causing great offence, I was invited in by the rabbi's wife and introduced to her *six* children, which made me wince and tense my thighs in sympathy. Then the stud himself, Rabbi Strochenberg, emerged from his office, enthusiastically shook me by the hand and ushered me in.

'Come in, come in!' he said, smiling broadly. 'Sorry to keep you waiting; I was on the phone to yet another soon-to-be divorcee. There seems to be an epidemic of divorces in the community right now.'

So I guess touching another man's wife wasn't that uncommon, after all.

'Oh,' I said, looking around the room at the shelves heaving with books on Judaism, one of which he wiggled out of its place wedged between two weightier tomes and gave to me.

'But don't worry,' he said with that twinkle in his eye. 'I have a good feeling about you two.'

And so he went on cheerily advising me on what made a good marriage from a Jewish perspective, imparting wisdom fed down from countless generations of Jews. Such as the fact that it was a *mitzvah* (that's a good thing) to 'satisfy' your wife on a regular basis. 'Well, mate,' I thought, 'you're preaching to the choir there, for sure.' I mean, ever since Sasithorn Sonjohnkoksoong had shown me how, it was never a chore for me to 'satisfy' a lady – my God, it was basically my raison d'être. Not only did it feel bloody great, it was one method I had employed to distract my girlfriends from remembering they were going out with a total dweeb.

Another law of marriage Rabbi Strochenberg imparted during those meetings was that the wedding must not take place when the bride is on her period. 'Sheesh!' I thought, my heart sinking somewhat. 'As if coordinating the caterers, the room hire, the car hire, the diaries of the rabbi with ours and that of our nearest and dearest wasn't hard enough, we now have to liaise with Jo's uterus wall as well.'

Despite my inner wobble at such menstrual matters, Strochenberg's eyes lit up during our meetings, I think because I showed such a sincere interest in the traditions and culture I was reconnecting with. But my fascination was only really the kind I would have on discovering more about the process behind making a tin of baked beans or the latest aftershave when I had to be involved in marketing them to the public. I was mainly, and happily, doing all this to please Jo's parents. And let's face it, when has a wedding ever been about what the bride or groom really want? I'm afraid my enthusiasm for learning new things may have lulled Strochenberg into thinking he had a malleable soul on his hands, one who was ready to embrace the orthodox ways, when in fact I was stopping by McDonald's on my way home from meetings with him – I don't know why, but there was something about all that talk of Basar BeChalav (that's the forbidden mixing of dairy with meat, for all the uninitiated among you) that made me crave a quarter-pounder with cheese.

'Hey, Jo,' I said as I got home to our flat after one of those meetings, near-empty Maccy D's paper bag in hand.

'Hey. You're late,' she said. 'Where have you been? My parents are here.'

'Really?' I said, the blood draining from my body as I poked my head around the living room door to see Paul and Rachel perched on the sofa nursing cups of tea. I quickly rugby-passed the bag to Jo and she chucked it in the kitchen bin, before following me into the lounge where I could proudly excuse my lateness because I had been meeting with Rabbi Strochenberg, although I always sounded like someone in need of a good dose of Lemsip whenever I said his name.

'Oh that's nice, isn't it, Paul?' Rachel said – I'm sure she was referring to my conference with the rabbi rather than my phlegmy attempt at pronouncing his moniker.

'Very good,' Paul said, looking like he was desperate to go to the toilet, but then God knows how many cups of tea he'd had whilst waiting for me.

'So what brings you here?' I said. 'Not that it isn't lovely to see you of—'

'You did,' Paul said rather impatiently.

'I did what?'

'Brought us here.'

'Me?'

'Yes,' Jo cut in. 'You know. We wanted to tell Mum and Dad that thing.'

'That thing?'

'Yes that thing, you know.' Jo's eyes widened as she tried desperately to speak telepathically to my stupid brain.

'That thing… that thing,' I mused. 'Oh! *That* thing.' The penny dropped at last. 'Was that today?'

'Yes, did you forget?'

Blanked it out more like. 'Oh, it must have slipped my mind. But we don't need to bother them with that now. We can talk about that, erm, next week sometime.'

'Noooooh, James,' Jo sang.

'Tomorrow?'

'Noooooh.'

'First thing tomorrow?'

She shook her head.

'Second thing tomorrow?'

?

'Later on? We could have a drink first,' I said, heading for the cupboard where I kept the spirits.

'No!'

'Now?'

Jo nodded and looked at her parents, who had been following our little dialogue with their heads like spectators at a tennis match, at night, with no floodlighting.

'OK,' Jo said, and sat next to her parents on the sofa while I took the armchair, expecting the straps and the hood and the wet sponge and the electrodes to be applied at any moment. 'There's something we need to tell you about James.' I flinched and Jo clarified, 'About James's dad actually.'

'OK, go on,' Paul said warily.

'Before I go on, please no knee-jerk reaction, OK? Mum?'

Rachel nodded quickly, eager for her daughter to just get to the point.

'Dad?'

'Yes, yes,' he said with understandable irritation.

'Well, what is it, darling?'

'Well, before I start, you need to know, James and his dad *are* Jewish.'

They seemed to breathe a synchronised sigh of relief, but I might have just imagined that.

Jo took a deep breath, 'But I'm afraid James's dad… he's in prison. For drug dealing.'

'Really?' Paul said, with a hint of morbid fascination in his tone. But as soon as Jo confirmed it with a nod his tone became more sombre. 'Oh. Dear.'

'That's terrible,' said Rachel.

Flick the switch now, executioner, for God's sake!

'I'm so sorry, *we're* so sorry for not telling you sooner, but you know I really love James and I was worried you'd tell me to stop seeing him. He was in a very dark place – James's dad, not James – you see, he'd just lost his wife to cancer and he'd come out as gay, but kind of went down the wrong path—'

'You what? He's gay as well? But how can he—?'

'It's a long story, Mum, but the point is… Are you OK with all this?'

The pause that followed was Pinter porn.

Then finally Jo's mum piped up. 'Well… as long as you're happy with James, darling…'

What? No teacups flying through the air? No biscuits being choked upon? No gouging my eyes out with teaspoons? No milk being spilt? No! It seems even if there had been, Paul and Rachel saw no point in crying over it – as long as it wasn't Basar BeChalav, of course. And as we all embraced, Jo and I looked at each other like two newborns squinting in the light of this unexpectedly comforting new world.

CHAPTER 33

TISH, TISH!

'I'm on my period.'

It was our wedding day.

'What?'

'It's my time of the month.'

'WHAT?'

'I'm menstruating. Arsenal are playing at home. The Red Sea is flowing.'

'OK, OK, I get it! But you can't be.'

'Erm… My vagina begs to differ there, James.'

'Oh no. I thought we had it all worked out. The dates and…'

'Well, Mother Nature had other ideas, clearly.'

'Does this mean… What does this mean? Do we have to cancel?'

'I am not cancelling this wedding, James.'

'But the rabbi said—'

'Well, if Rabbi Strochenberg wants to have a word with my uterus he's welcome to, but if he does I think he'll come away with more than egg on his face.'

'OK, OK. Let's just keep it quiet then, yeah?'

'I have no intention of broadcasting it.'

I hung up, but I couldn't shake the feeling that this was not a good omen. I turned on the radio. A bit of Queen or The Darkness was what I needed right then. I got Leona Lewis, 'Bleeding Love'. I turned off the radio.

The buzzer rang. Jo's dad was here. We were being driven to the wedding together. This, and my raging hangover, didn't ease my sense of dread at all, but then my mobile rang.

'Dad?'

'Son?'

'You OK?'

'I'm OK. You?'

I felt the tears welling up. 'I'm good, yeah.' It was so good to hear his voice.

'Congratulations, son, on today. I'm so proud of you.'

'Thanks, Dad,' I said, then stopped myself from saying, 'Wish you were here.' I really did wish he was here, but I reckoned saying it might just make him feel worse than he already did about being stuck in Wormwood Scrubs, where he now resided, on my wedding day – but looking on the bright side, at least he couldn't be late.

'Where are you now?'

'Getting in the car. On the way to the shul. With Paul.'

'Jo's father?'

'Yes.'

'Can I speak to him?'

'Really?' That sense of dread was suddenly back.

'Of course.'

'OK,' I said, handing the phone over reluctantly to Paul, who looked a little nervous to take it.

'Hello?' Paul said cautiously.

And then he listened. And so did I, as hard as I could, but I couldn't hear a bloody thing my dad was saying, of course. I could only guess what he might be saying by Paul's responses. This was the first time they had ever spoken to each other, but not the first time Paul had seen my dad. Although Dad had been securely locked behind the walls of one prison or another since shortly after meeting Jo, her parents got a rare opportunity to see him via the magic of television when my dad made an appearance on *Question Time* with David Dimbleby – not sitting on the panel, I hasten to add, but as part of the studio audience, peppered as it was with inmates of the Scrubs, from where the programme was coming that week. Dad was part of a select few cons who were actually allowed to ask questions too, I assume because he was 'doing well' there – a phrase which I always found rather dubious in this context. But Dad had told me during one phone call that he had been moved to the nicest part of the prison – the West Wing, a name which sent images scudding across my mind of him in a suit lording it up behind a desk in a cell which looked remarkably like the Oval Office as his convict minions ran in and out delivering him tea and biscuits and getting him to sign the latest government bill.

'It's like getting a free upgrade at a hotel,' he'd said. Only my dad could see it in such terms. 'Oh, 'sup, Bulldog!'

'What was that, Dad?'

'Oh, nothing, just saying hello to one of the other guys.'

'Sup, Bulldog? Did he really just say *'sup*? Perhaps I misheard. The line was pretty shitty. But I could've sworn that it was followed immediately by the jangly sound of him fist-bumping the bling-laden hand of said Bulldog. Nah! You misheard that as well, I told myself. I don't think bling is even allowed in prison anyway. But then again, once you get *upgraded* perhaps you get all sorts of other privileges too. Or perhaps Bulldog can do what the fuck he likes, mainly 'cause his name is Bulldog and you don't get a name like that if you're a pussy.

Those images of big fists had me recalling Alfie the Bear, ex-con and mate of Dad's, who'd supplied me with pills back in 2002. How times had changed! Just before he went down, Dad's drug business had made Alfie's look like a school tuck shop. So when Dad described himself as *doing well* inside perhaps he meant that, with the assistance of his new receptionist and henchman Bulldog, Dad was busy making himself rich and indispensable to screws and cons alike by supplying them with the best meth a prison kitchen can cook up.

But before I could let my imagination not only run away with me, but lock me in the boot of its car and drive me to a private jetty where it bundled me onto a boat and left me on a desert island from which I had no hope of ever getting back, I consoled myself with the idea that Her Majesty wouldn't be letting such a remorseless offender represent her penal system on the BBC. No, I'm sure Dad was selected as he was a shining example of reform. And as the camera panned across to where his balding pate did indeed shine under the studio lights (no pre-show make-up for the audience, clearly), I felt a thrilling mix of dread and pride (not, ironically, unlike the rush off an E) as my local bad penny dad was addressed by national treasure Dimbleby.

'And I think, yes, we now have one of the inmates who has a question. Yes, you, sir, in the blue jumper.' Prison-issue blue jumper, that was.

'Oh yes, thank you,' the little bald man said politely. He was thin, but not as emaciated as he had been at the height of his addiction. He looked less stressed, healthier, a lot like my old dad in many ways, and the way he made the most of his little cameo in the show now added to that sense for me. 'When will we finally decide to leave the European Court of Justice? It's costing us a fortune.'

Of course, Dad. Of course, you would ask that! I smiled at the TV as I recalled him at the bargain bin in Tesco, triumphant that his trolley full of cereal would not be costing him a fortune that day.

The audience broke out into a round of applause with even the odd whoop of agreement thrown in while Kenneth Clarke, panellist and staunch Europhile, bristled and said, 'That is obviously separate from the EU and simply covers law. There is no connection with money blah blah blah…'

With a twinkle in his eye Dimbleby looked at my dad and said, 'You did that for a reaction, didn't you?'

Cut to Dad nodding and grinning, more cheeky school boy than dangerous drug baron.

I sat back on the sofa and muted the Labour politician on the panel trying to score points off Kenneth Clarke's irritation. 'That's my dad,' I said, an apologetic tone contrived to mask my pride in front of Paul and Rachel.

'Well,' Paul said, 'he seems to be a very nice man. Kind-looking.'

Of course, I thought. A crack-addict drug-baron. They must have been expecting Bulldog, not the little smiling senior citizen in the blue jumper.

'A nice, kind-looking Jewish man,' Rachel said, reassuring herself.

I had squeezed Jo's hand then, but now in the car on the way to our wedding her comforting presence was, obviously, elsewhere – in the bogs at the shul, no doubt, making sure her preferred item of feminine hygiene was securely in place. So I carried on watching Paul's responses as he spoke to Dad on the phone, trying to interpret his words.

'Oh, nice to speak to you… I know, it's certainly unusual… Mmm, well… never mind… there's nothing you could… these things happen…'

What things? Getting banged up for possession of the biggest haul of crystal meth in UK history? No, they don't. Well, they shouldn't. I was leaning towards the phone, willing my father not to say something stupid, or cast himself in a bad light, but as the two dads chatted away I realised there was absolutely nothing I could do about it. What he said, how he painted himself to Paul and to the world, was out of my control, and it was not for me to do it anyway. I needed to mind my own business and concentrate on how I presented myself to the world.

Ever since my little family unit had fractured when I was just nineteen and I had scolded my parents for it, before I realised why they needed to part ways, I had been trying to do the impossible: I had been trying to stop things from changing. As soon as a bunch of individuals get together and call themselves a family they are attempting the impossible: forcing their mutable selves into an immutable unit, and it can only end in tears. If I believe that, I hear you ask, then why the hell was I right then about to force a new little impossibility into existence, i.e. Mr and Mrs James Lubbock and whatever kids came our way? Well, it also occurred to me on that journey (both the car journey and the one I'd been on for the last decade or so) that there was hope for those individuals in a family unit if they are allowed – if they allow each other – to grow and change. And in the light of this notion I held out hope for myself, and so to add to the vows I'd be taking that day, I made another silent one as we drove through North Finchley that wasn't in the rabbi's text: I vow to let each soul in my family grow and change and be whoever the hell they want to be, whoever the hell they need to be.

Despite my fears, the wedding went well – it was a big fat Jewish wedding, and because the United shul was involved, there was more to it than the average Jewish wedding: there were more prayers; there was lots more Jewish dancing; the rabbi, his wife and the *chazzan* (the lead singer in the shul) were invited to the party; and then there was the Tish. I hadn't the faintest idea what a Tish was, but I started to like the look of it when I saw large jugs of whisky being brought to the table. The point was to officially sign the wedding contract, but essentially it was just a big Jewish piss-up – men only, of course. But apart from this misogynistic detail, after a jug or two I was well on my way before the party proper had even started, aided by the relentless dancing, orchestrated with gusto by Rabbi Strochenberg, during which I was endlessly flung about, hands were clapped, feet were stomped, and we danced, danced, danced in circles until I was ready to puke. But thankfully soon it was time for the speeches and I could have a long relaxing sit down – that was until I remembered that, as well as Elliot, Jake was my best man.

'Why exactly did I make Jake my best man?' I asked myself as he got up, ran his hand through the Jewfro and began to regale the assembled crowd – half of which were of course Jo's family, my new family, family who I had yet to meet properly – in his inimitably erratic style with tales about all those crazy adventures we'd had over all the years we'd known each other, including, of course, nearly getting arrested that time in America after losing control of the car, and my part in tying him naked to a lamppost before he left for the States. Since many other moments in our lives together involved copious amounts of booze and drugs I was understandably jittery, but pleasantly surprised that he managed to avoid most of those, and I was moved by some of the more touching things he said about us.

'I love James like a brother,' he said and the audience aahed appropriately. 'But not as much as James loves a McDonald's quarter-pounder with cheese, eh, James?'

The audience at this decidedly kosher wedding visibly cringed as one at my decidedly unkosher choices, not, as might be more appropriate, at my penchant for consuming the shit that that corporate monster passes as food. I looked over at Rabbi Strochenberg, who had been positively beaming all day, but now his face was that of a little boy who'd just been told his holiday to Disneyland was cancelled five minutes before departure and that instead he was about to get on a plane to Romania where there were apparently some lovely orphanages. The rabbi had had such high hopes for me after all those cosy little meetings in his office. But now, as the scales fell from his eyes, he could see I was a lost cause.

I blamed Jo's period.

CHAPTER 34
CONEHEADS

Jo became pregnant so soon after the honeymoon that I revelled in my evident virility – until, that was, the realities of pregnancy stomped all over it. Given my family life over the past ten years or so, I shouldn't have been surprised that the realities of this pregnancy were not the normal realities of pregnancy. There were complications. Plenty of the little bastards. The first came at the three-month check, when it was discovered the foetus had more fluid than expected behind its neck. This pointed to a significantly increased risk of conditions such as Down's Syndrome and heart abnormalities. However, after a few nerve-racking months, after tests and close-up heart scans, we were relieved to hear everything was fine, and we could expect a healthy baby after all. One–nil to me, complications!

It was then a question of waiting, watching the bump grow, having a mild panic that the baby had stopped moving, then an hour or so later seeing Jo's belly undulate like John Hurt's in *Alien*, much to our enormous relief. The emotional rollercoaster was ongoing, fuelled by paranoia after that early scare. As I watched Jo watching with wonder and trepidation as her own body changed, I couldn't help but see my own mum as a young woman watching the bulge that would one day become me. She would have had the same wonder on her face now to see her first grandchild developing, but none of the trepidation, I reckoned, as she would be an old hand at this parenting business. 'God, she would have been handy to have around now,' I thought, and it was my chest's turn to do the John Hurt thing as my heart throbbed with missing her.

You may remember that I – how did I put it in Chapter One? – *never liked surprises, not in real life anyway*. I suppose after all that had happened since then, all the surprises and shocks, I should have been impervious to them now. At least that's how my character would probably have grown to be if he were to conform to the formula of a 'good' movie. But I'm afraid that wasn't the case. Certainly not where this pregnancy was concerned. When Jo reached full term I could hardly bear the anticipation any longer. So in order to get the little Jewish bugger delivered into the world, I suggested we get a hot Indian curry delivered to the door, as I'd heard that was supposed to *loosen things up*. And sure enough, the next evening Jo's contractions began.

My bowels were suddenly loosened too, though I couldn't tell if that was the vindaloo or the sheer panic. We sped to the hospital only to be sent away like greedy schoolkids at the serving hatch too early for dessert. Jo was not dilated enough, apparently, although I probably was. So there we were, back at home waiting in limbo, in no-man's land, which felt terribly appropriate to me as someone who had been called a man by society since I was eighteen, but who always felt like a child just zipping himself into an older skin every year – a thirteen-year-old still looking out from beneath all those older-looking layers. No-man's land, no-father's land, but no-boy's land either – how could we pass the time in this purgatory? Box sets, of course! If I'd have had my way it would probably have been *Star Trek*, but given that Jo was the one who was actually dealing directly with this pregnancy thing, I thought it only fair to let her choose. So *Homeland* it was. We binge-watched virtually the entire series, Jo clutching my hand periodically as her contractions came and went, me clutching hers as CIA agent Carrie Mathison met with yet another cliffhanger.

We fell asleep exhausted after all those cliffhangers, and the next morning went back to the hospital sure that now Jo would qualify as *dilated enough*. But the nurses weren't so sure. First they noticed the baby's heart rate dramatically dropped during each contraction, then Jo's blood pressure was measured as too high, which was diagnosed as early pre-eclampsia. One–all, complications! The dilation was taking hours to reach the desired measurement and things were still not ready to go by midnight – this baby did not want to come out into the world.

And I couldn't blame it. What trials and tribulations, shocks, surprises, losses and gains, highs and lows lay in wait for it out here that we, its parents, couldn't protect it from no matter how many layers of proverbial cotton wool we wrapped it in? And how many of those tribulations might we be directly responsible for... might *I* be directly responsible for? It was all I could do then not to climb into Jo's womb with the baby and hide from this unpredictable nonsense we call life. I wasn't ready to be a father! I mean, whenever I looked at the ultrasound scans I just saw the shape of the USS *Enterprise*, which drove it home what a child I still was, always would be. I should be sitting in my boxers watching reruns of *Star Trek* and playing *Getaway* on the PlayStation with Jake and Will, not being called 'the father' and sharing total responsibility for another human being with Jo. No wonder my own dad went off the rails – I'm surprised he waited until my nineteenth birthday and didn't start jacking up on the day I was born.

I looked desperately around the consulting room for a cupboard full of morphine or something that I could abuse, but suddenly the doctor was calling for a 'crash delivery' and there was a whirlwind of activity as Jo was pushed into an operating theatre. I had no idea what a crash delivery was, but it clearly wasn't good. I found myself handed scrubs to wear and before you could say 'I better go and check if I left the gas on' I was standing in the theatre feeling somewhat surplus to requirements as doctors and nurses buzzed around Jo, and rather nauseated at watching her sliced open. I was informed that the baby's heart rate had dropped to dangerous levels, but, the doctor smiled at me, it was improving. Improving? It was probably racing now, I thought, if it could see those medieval-looking forceps the doctor was brandishing. It was unsurprising to me that the baby was not prepared to be pulled out of the womb by a giant pair of nutcrackers, so a caesarean section was ordered.

'You might want to sit down for this bit,' I was told.

I didn't argue. A good move, as it turned out, as after fifteen long minutes I saw a tiny, blood-soaked creature pulled from Jo which, although it looked like something from *Coneheads*, was the most beautiful thing I had ever seen.

'Dad, this is Mia.'

Dad beamed and cooed over my four-month-old daughter and we blinked at each other with all the breathless amazement of tsunami survivors. I had had no doubt that becoming a grandfather would be as significant to my dad as becoming a father was to me, and something which a few years ago he may have thought he wouldn't live long enough to see, but it didn't feel quite like the Hollywood ending I had been hoping for. Perhaps that was simply because we were sitting in the visiting room of a prison and my baby daughter had just been frisked as thoroughly as I had by the screws.

Jo and I had travelled down to Dorset for this visit since Dad had been transferred from Wormwood Scrubs to The

Verne, a category C prison on the Isle of Portland. I think this was another example of Dad *doing well*, but since this prison was in such a picturesque location by a popular holiday destination for avid sailors and people interested in water sports, I couldn't help feeling it might feel like more of a punishment with all that natural beauty just out of reach. I mean, at least in the Scrubs with the urban shithole that is Acton over the wall, you could tell yourself you were better off inside.

'Did you bring any cash in, James?'

'Yeah, they only let us bring in fifteen quid though, in coins.' I started to fish it out of my pocket and slide it across the table.

'You keep hold of it. Money's not much good to us in here.' I didn't like the way he kept saying 'us' all the time, as if he was the same as all these other criminals sitting at their tables chatting to their families. However, as I looked around the room I didn't see the shade-wearing, tattoo-clad mafia dons and henchmen I'd expected. All I saw were boringly normal-looking people. Just people trying to navigate the pitfalls of life, who had made stupid mistakes and were now paying for them, trying to rebuild – in many ways just like my dad. (I suppose Bulldog didn't have any visitors that day.) 'But would you get me some chocolate from the vending machine? I have to stay sitting here.'

'I'll go,' Jo said.

'Thanks, Jo.'

'Sweets and burn…' he said.

'Burn?'

'Tobacco. Tobacco and sweets, that's the official currency in here.'

'Currency?'

'Yeah, some people in here make a business out of the old double bubble.'

'Double bubble?'

'Yeah, they get some burn in their canteen every week to lend out.'

'Canteen?' I swear he was throwing all these words in on purpose just to mess with my head.

'Canteen is like your shopping order you get once a week. You can get most things if you can afford it from your prison account. Sweets, fruit, cereal, cocoa, lighters, Rizla, tobacco, anything. But five half-ounce packs of burn is your weekly limit. So plenty of guys who smoke don't have any to trade.'

'What would they need to trade it for, Dad?'

Dad shrugged coyly. 'Drugs. See, a small bag of smack will cost you five packs of burn. Now, if you've already smoked half your weekly allowance then you'll need to borrow some off someone else before all the smack gets snapped up. And trust me, it'll get snapped up quickly too.'

I felt as if I had popped into the bank only to pass through a portal to a parallel universe where Dad was the bank manager explaining the latest alien interest rates.

'So they borrow the burn. But when it comes to burn it's double bubble, i.e. for every five packs of burn you borrow you pay back ten when you get it.'

'That's a hundred per cent interest!'

'Yeah, good, eh?' Some things never changed, and Dad revelling in a good deal was one of those things. 'Well, good for the lenders anyway. But it's bloody hard to get out of that kind of debt once you're in. You have to borrow more and more each week to fund your habit and pay off your debt, and so it spirals and spirals.'

Although what he said reminded me of my own credit card bill, I looked at Dad disapprovingly. 'Dad, you're not one of these lenders, are you?' Perhaps my fears about him and Bulldog weren't so far-fetched after all.

Dad looked at me for a moment, then laughed. 'God no, son! I haven't got time for all that. What with teaching English classes, coaching the football team and helping out in counselling sessions, I've never been busier actually.'

Jo returned with the chocolate and Dad cradled it for a moment, almost as lovingly as he had Mia. Then he gorged on a Mars Bar and I smiled like he used to as I stuffed French fries into my gob when he took me out to McDonald's after waiting for him to finish work at his little shop in Regent Street all those years ago.

CHAPTER 35

HAPPY BIRTHDAY

Winter 2013. Dad was released after serving nearly four years of his eight-year sentence. He had turned out to be the model prisoner. Just as he said, he had kept himself busy, helped other prisoners with learning and coping strategies and gained many inmates' admiration for all the right reasons. And, crucially, he had no interest in drugs – dealing or taking – anymore. He was a shining example of how the penal system can work for some people.

This was of course something to be celebrated, and what better way to do so than by having him come to Jo's parents' house for dinner – yes, I was being sarcastic: I was full of trepidation for that day when it finally came around. This would be the first time he would actually meet Jo's family in the flesh. And they would all be there, of course. Grandma, Rob who was still in marble, and Jo's sister with that knowing smile (what did she know this time? I thought all my skeletons were not only out of the closet, but parading down the street in sparkly gold hot pants, toking on a crack pipe and waving a rainbow flag). But what exactly filled me with such anxiety? As far I knew, Dad was completely clean now so it wasn't like I feared him racking up a line on their coffee table or offering Grandma a go on his meth pipe. In many ways he was back to his old self... Ah! That was what I was worried about.

'You look amazing for your age,' he said to Jo's mum. 'You could turn me, you know.'

Everyone around the table cringed, much like they did at Jake's best man speech. I thought I heard Grandma mutter, 'The apple doesn't fall far from the tree,' but my Hebrew is rubbish so it might just have been, 'Pass the apple sauce!'

'Have you been to the opera recently, Dad?' I said, quickly trying to show everyone that despite that last comment, he was in fact very cultured. And in truth he had been spending some of his pension on going to the opera again, on classical music concerts and the ballet – and downloading the odd trance *choon*, but we didn't need to talk about that here.

'Oh, yes. I went to see the ENO's *Magic Flute* last week. Beautifully done.'

'Really?' Rachel said. 'So you recommend it?'

'Oh, yes. You should take your wife, Paul. Or I might have to.' He laughed.

No one else did.

'Pass the butter, Dad!' I said quickly.

'You heard the rumour going around about the butter?' he said.

Everyone looked blankly at Dad.

'Never mind,' he grinned. 'I shouldn't spread it.'

'Oh, Dad,' I groaned, my mirthless laugh meant to show somehow to the assembled in-laws that my father was not the font of all rubbish jokes, but in fact a master of irony.

I drank half a glass of wine in one go and thought about downing the rest when he said – and he was deadly serious now: 'Rachel, where do you get your bread?'

'Oh, I got this from Waitrose.'

'You can get just as good a loaf from Tesco, you know. And it's over a pound cheaper.'

'Oh,' Rachel tried to sound as if she cared.

'And if you time it just right, you can snap it up just after they reduce it to half price. And it's still good for a few days, whatever it says on the label.

'Oh, well… I shall bear that in mind, Richard.'

'And if you're looking for cereal—'

'Dad,' I cut in, otherwise in a matter of minutes he'd be dragging my mother-in-law round Tesco filling her trolley with cut-price Shredded Wheat. 'Have you seen any of your old friends recently? In the coin business or…'

'Oh, that's right,' Paul said, 'You were a dealer… I mean a coin dealer before, weren't you?'

'Yes. I was,' Dad said. 'I even went to the London Coin Show the other day, but I realised my heart wasn't in it anymore. And besides, it's not like I have any money to invest in it now. I knew nearly everyone there though. That was a bit weird, you know, since they all knew how... let's say, how I *diversified* my business over the years.'

Jo's sister sniggered.

'So, to answer your question, son, no, I don't see many of my old friends from that world these days. There's just a couple of good ones I keep in touch with still. And I made a few friends inside who are actually lovely blokes. Bulldog, for examp—'

'What about Aunty Julie? You still see her, don't you?' I said, straining to sound curious. I knew damn well he saw his sister. Every other Sunday. And I knew they had a masochistically tempestuous relationship, to put it mildly, but I suspected the in-laws would rather hear about that than Bulldog and Dad's other ex-con mates at this moment in time.

'Oh, don't get me started on Julie!' Dad said.

As much as I wanted to get him started on Julie, Paul, it seemed, didn't and said, 'How are you finding Poplar, Richard?'

'Well, it's OK. I'm not saying the flat is too small, but my cell in Wormwood Scrubs was more roomy.'

He laughed. Paul and Rachel managed a squeak of appreciation for that one. Rob's face looked as if it was set in marble.

'No, no, it's fine really,' he said and he looked down at his plate for the first time in many minutes.

As a result of the confiscation proceedings Dad had lost everything. No more gold Roller, no luxury apartments, not even the old Cortina. He now lived in a small, one-bed flat in

Poplar paid for by his housing benefit and punishingly close to the luxury flats he once owned in Limehouse. The last time I visited those flats a couple of years after his arrest, the thing that struck me among the detritus left there was those bloody Tesco carrier bags he used to keep his essentials in, before he upgraded to that khaki man-bag. Now the Tesco bags were nothing but a pile of shredded, decomposing plastic lying by the mattress on his bedroom floor. Time had taken its toll on them, just as it had on him, changing him from Earl Grey to Mr Big and back again. But new life can come from decaying things. And in the spirit of that cycle Dad had not only rekindled his love of the arts, but he spent much of his remaining pension spoiling his two grandchildren (two now, yes! I really was a virile stallion, after all – not to Rabbi Strochenberg's standards, but two's good enough for me). He spends nearly every weekend with Mia and Gracie. He really is a devoted granddad. No control over them whatsoever, but at least he's there for them.

'That was a lovely meal, Rachel,' I said, getting up to take some plates out to the kitchen like a good son-in-law.

'Don't worry, I'll do that,' Paul said.

'No, no,' I insisted.

'Yes, let Paul do it,' Rachel said. 'He needs the exercise.'

Dad laughed at Rachel's little joke and I prayed he wouldn't say she was so funny that he might turn hetero for her, yet again.

'And while you're at it,' Rachel said. 'Why don't you put the kettle on?'

'Well, I would,' Paul said, 'but I'm afraid it won't fit.'

Perhaps I imagined it, but everything stopped for a moment then and I found myself back in our semi in Stanmore. I was a kid, Dad was just a coin dealer and Mum was groaning at his bad joke about putting the kettle on. It was an elevator-drop moment for my stomach, but as Dad and Paul began cracking up at each other's favourite bad gag, I felt a kind of relief I hadn't felt in a long time. And when Paul returned from the kitchen with a birthday cake and the lights were dimmed and they all sang Happy Birthday for Dad, I really felt like I'd got a bit of that Hollywood ending I'd so foolishly hoped for back in HMP The Verne. I could see it meant the world to Dad too. And I wondered what a stranger who'd read the newspaper headlines on the day my dad was sent down would think now if they could see this *drug baron* before us. This journey has made me think twice when I read the headlines today. Be it *drug baron* or *terrorist*, what is the real story behind the label? What makes a drug baron become one? What makes a terrorist deserve that title?

Dad went off the rails because he lost his rock: Mum. Not when they separated – that was all part of his chance to flourish, to become his true self. He still had Mum in his life then and that was a very grounding thing for him and just what he needed in the giddy heights of his new-found sexuality. If anyone could relate to him, despite their different paths, it must have been Mum, as she forged a new life with Ruth. So it was when Mum died that he truly floundered. And I too could've gone off the rails with him at one point there, if it hadn't been for my very own rock, Jo.

This week I zip myself into a forty-year-old's skin. How the hell did that happen? These days this little thirteen-year-old geek plays the part of the husband, the father, the responsible breadwinner. So still, by my dad's standards, there's plenty of time to go nuts, become the don of an international crime syndicate, run a porn empire, deal heroin, or even deal in marble, or perhaps just stay a software consultant, as I am now. But whatever I do, whatever I become, I'll always be the son too – son to the best mum a little soldier could wish for, and to a dad who's made some mistakes, some whoppers in fact, but who I admire eternally every day for having the strength of spirit to come out to the world and be proud of who he really is.

ACKNOWLEDGEMENTS

JAMES

First and foremost I want to pay tribute to my wife Jo, who has kept me grounded, provided the support when I needed it most and still somehow manages to spin countless plates – I wouldn't have been able to do it without you x

To Mum – I'll miss you always. Thank you for making me the person I am today and for your unending love.

To Ruth, without whom I'm not sure how I would have coped during Mum's illness – I will never forget your incredible fortitude and love during that time, and cherish the wonderful relationship we have now.

To my wife's family: my parents-in-law, sister and brother-in-law – thank you for your warmth and humour, and for accepting me and making me feel so welcome despite the baggage I carried!

To all my close friends, The Group, and others who have always been there for me, who always make me laugh and to whom I am eternally grateful for your friendships.

To Warren, without whom this book would not have happened. Thank you for believing in my story, applying your great talent to making it special and doubling up as an agent extraordinaire!

To Ajda and the team at Mirror Books, for your passion, enthusiasm and vision – I loved every minute working with you.

A special mention to Nick Tarlton and Mike Golding, to whom the title of this book owes a debt of gratitude.

And last but not least, I guess I have to thank the old man – we've been through a hell of a lot together, but I'm so glad we managed to come out the other end and still retain our sanities!

WARREN

Top thanks to James for trusting me with your story and allowing me to mine the light from some very dark crevices.

Also huge thanks to you, Richard, who took this version of events on the chin as you have everything the English judicial system has thrown at you since your arrest.

Thanks to all James's family and friends for being so cooperative and for understanding that real life has to be squashed and bent a little here and there to fit into the box of a good read.

Thanks to Ajda Vucicevic at Mirror Books for your sharp editorial eye, your sensitivity and for making me work harder!

And to my loved ones – yes, you! – love, lots of.

James Lubbock was born and raised in North West London. He studied English Literature, Economics and History at school before following his passion at Bournemouth University by focussing on film and TV production. He specialised in new media and began his career first as a programmer, then found his way into digital marketing.

He now works in the software industry consulting on social media platforms and technology. In his spare time, he's an avid Arsenal supporter, keen amateur astronomer, and enjoys running half marathons to stay fit. He is happily married with children.

Warren FitzGerald was born in 1973 and now lives in London. His debut novel *The Go-Away Bird*, published in 2010, won an Amazon Rising Stars Award, was Waterstones' Book of the Month for October 2011, and was longlisted for The Authors' Club Best First Book Award. Warren's first non-fiction work *All in the Same Boat* has been optioned for the screen, scheduled for production in 2019.

Since graduating from Warwick University, he has also been a professional singer and worked with children and adults with disabilities. He has undertaken voluntary projects overseas including building a health centre in Kibungo, Rwanda (the setting for *The Go-Away Bird*).